THE GREAT NARRATIVE

Klaus Schwab
Thierry Malleret

FORUM PUBLISHING

Edition 1.0

World Economic Forum
91-93 route de la Capite
CH-1223 Cologny/Geneva
Switzerland
Tel.: +41 (0)22 869 1212
Fax: +41 (0)22 786 2744
mail: contact@weforum.org
www.weforum.org

ISBN 978-2-940631-30-8

About the authors

Professor **Klaus Schwab** (1938, Ravensburg, Germany) is the Founder and Executive Chairman of the World Economic Forum. In 1971, he published *Modern Enterprise Management in Mechanical Engineering*. He argues in that book that a company must serve not only shareholders but all stakeholders to achieve long-term growth and prosperity. To promote the stakeholder concept, he founded the World Economic Forum the same year.

Professor Schwab holds doctorates in Economics (University of Fribourg) and in Engineering (Swiss Federal Institute of Technology) and obtained a master's degree in Public Administration (MPA) from the Kennedy School of Government at Harvard University. In 1972, in addition to his leadership role at the Forum, he became a professor at the University of Geneva. He has since received numerous international and national honours, including 17 honorary doctorates. His latest books are ***The Fourth Industrial Revolution*** (2016), a worldwide bestseller translated into 30 languages, and ***Shaping the Future of the Fourth Industrial Revolution*** (2018).

Thierry Malleret (1961, Paris, France) is the Managing Partner of the Monthly Barometer, a succinct predictive analysis provided to private investors, global CEOs and opinion and decision-makers. His professional experience includes founding the Global Risks Network at the World Economic Forum and heading its Programme team.

Malleret was educated at the Sorbonne and the Ecole des Hautes Etudes en Sciences Sociales, Paris, and at St Antony's College, Oxford. He holds master's degrees in Economics and History, and a PhD in Economics. His career spans investment banking, think tanks, academia and government (with a three-year spell in the prime minister's office in Paris). He has written several business and academic books and has published four novels. He lives in Chamonix, France, with his wife Mary Anne.

Contents

Foreword

We live in times of unprecedented change and have, as never before, the responsibility and potential to build a better future together.

Times of unprecedented change, with major economic, environmental, geopolitical, societal and technological challenges that coincide and amplify each other, require unprecedented action. Premised on the belief that we have both a responsibility and the potential to respond to these issues, *The Great Narrative* is a call to collective and individual action. The thinking behind the book is inspired by a profound conviction that to ensure a better future for humankind, the world needs to be more resilient, more equitable and more sustainable.

In *COVID 19: The Great Reset*, published in July 2020, we raised the curtain on these issues. *The Great Narrative* places a cast of possible solutions to them on centre stage. What the epilogue to our human saga will be will depend on which narrative prevails.

Why do narratives matter? As human beings and social animals, we are storytelling creatures, and the stories we tell (the narratives) are our fundamental tool of communication and transmission. Narratives are how we make sense of life; they provide us with a context, thanks to which we can better interpret, understand and respond to the facts we observe. Most importantly, compelling narratives have the power to inspire us to act. But why a single great narrative? Because the constellation of important interrelated stories that this book offers coalesce around one central story. It addresses a broad spectrum of issues aiming to shed light on what's coming and to offer some clarity on our options in terms of a collective response. Even so, *The Great Narrative* proposes a framework for future action, not a prescription.

The Great Narrative expresses our personal convictions about the best way forward. We recognize that the problems we collectively face are considerable, but we also believe that solutions do exist and are within our grasp. In that sense, it is a hopeful book that categorically rejects the doomsday mindset consigning humanity to a future of oblivion. Human creativity, ingenuity and innate sociality are much too powerful for that and can prevail.

Our views and convictions are informed by our humanistic values: the book is evidence-based and informed by science. It is also underpinned by 50 conversations that took place with foremost global thinkers and opinion-makers representing a variety of academic disciplines and points of view. Some corroborated our convictions. Others challenged them. All enriched our thinking. We are grateful to them.

15 December 2021

Klaus Schwab
Thierry Malleret

1. Introduction

What future do we face?
What future do we want?
What must we do to get there?

These three questions preoccupy us all. *The Great Narrative* provides a response to the first two and lays the foundations to address the third. We can't predict the future. However, we can imagine it and even design it; no outcome is predetermined and, as cognitive human beings, we retain the agency to shape the world we want. Perhaps most critically, we can also prepare for the future, by confronting both the risks that we can mitigate and the things that will surprise us.

The pandemic was one such thing. Many international organizations and individuals had warned for years that a pandemic would occur but, despite this, it took most of the world by complete surprise. Now (in December 2021), almost two years since it began, the pandemic seems never-ending and continues to drag on. We hope that the COVID-19 crisis will soon be over, but will it? "There is always a beginning and an end to every outbreak" as a former Director-General of the World Health Organization told us,[1] but pandemics as a social and psychological phenomenon are not episodic: they linger for years. A historian of science and medicine puts it this way: "We are living in the COVID-19 era, not the COVID-19 crisis. There will be a lot of changes that are substantial and persistent. We won't look back and say, 'That was a terrible time, but it's over.' We will be dealing with many of the ramifications of COVID-19 for decades."[2]

Indeed! Lessons from past pandemics tell us how hard it is to understand how, exactly when and why they end, and what their wide-ranging effects are. Throughout history, when the physical disease, measured in mortality or infection rates, subsides, the impact of the pandemic still remains. It continues to affect our lives, as economies and societies progressively adjust, and individuals strive to return to a semblance of normalcy. The psychological shock provoked by different forms of fear triggered by the disease – like the fear of illness, the fear of isolation, the fear of "others" or even the fear of the "future" – takes much longer to subside. It is already clear that the COVID-19 crisis has put into motion momentous changes that will unfold in a multifaceted fashion. Some of these changes were already apparent prior to the crisis but have been accelerated (even "turbo-charged", as some pundits would argue) by the pandemic. Among them are the acceleration of automation and innovation, rising inequalities, the growing power of tech and surveillance, the rising rivalry between the United

States and China, the partial retreat from globalization, the economic paradigm shift, and an increasingly fractious geopolitical landscape. But other changes now in the offing go beyond a mere acceleration of pre-existing trends, including a handful that would have seemed inconceivable before COVID-19 struck. The reconsideration of our social priorities (as expressed notably in the "Great Resignation" phenomenon), more radical welfare and taxation measures, new forms of state intervention, the rising appeal of well-being policies and a new appreciation for nature – these are just a few examples of new systemic changes that will grow in relevance.

Over the past millennia, pandemics have been the rule, not the exception. This being so, how can history help us understand what lies ahead? Pandemics are by nature a shock that divides and traumatizes. As such, they tend to exacerbate the same major issues and problems that have recurred throughout human history: wars and conflicts, inequalities and impoverishment, social cohesion and strife, political turbulence, the disruption of supply and demand, debt distress – to name a few notable ones. However, because of their inherently disruptive nature, pandemics can also prove to be a force for lasting and often radical change. COVID-19 is no exception. It has revealed, in a quasi-photographic manner, two things: (1) the main fault lines that beset today's world, like social divides, lack of fairness, limited cooperation, failure of global governance, geopolitical turmoil; but also (2) our extraordinary ability to mobilize and innovate when confronted with conditions of intense adversity. Who could have predicted back in the early days of the pandemic that so many governments and central banks would come to the rescue of their countries' societies and economies with such extraordinarily accommodative fiscal and monetary policies? Who could have imagined in the spring of 2020 that not one but several vaccines would be available less than a year later? A new world (not a "new normal") is now emerging, the contours of which will largely be defined by the narratives that evolve to inform and construct the way forward.

Throughout human history, this has been a key attribute of pandemics. They are an existential threat and, as such, they force us to think about the big questions, not only in relation to ourselves – our lives and our own mortality – but also vis-à-vis others. Pandemics serve as a big mirror held up to our collective "faces" that reflect back who we really are, both as individuals and societies. For this reason, like all deep crises, they force us to rethink the social contract that binds us together and the way we do things, which can in turn trigger innovation and pave the way for institutional, policy and societal ruptures. Momentous shocks (such as the one inflicted by the pandemic) can create momentous change, and dealing with adversity through the sheer power of ingenuity has always been part of our human condition. Why would it be different this time? It won't, except that two specific features of today's world will render the changes that are coming more abrupt, more complicated and more far-reaching than we might imagine.

1.1. Concatenation of risks and systemic connectivity

Interdependence – the by-product of technological progress and globalization – is the defining feature of the 21st century. It means that we live today on the brink of major consequential changes that are not independent from each other but are taking place simultaneously with their risks concatenated (i.e. linked together), reinforcing one another through cascading and contagion effects.[3] The pandemic has occurred at a very particular juncture when our economies and societies seem ill-suited to many of the challenges that lie ahead, when the geopolitical and technological landscapes are being reshaped in a way that will make them unrecognizable in just a few years, and when the environment is on the brink of disaster and climate change is an existential threat. The conjunction of all these challenges concurring simultaneously and impacting each other defines "systemic connectivity" and makes our current era unique in history: not only are all the changes happening at once, but they are also being exacerbated by the pandemic (and unfolding very fast). As we will see, solutions to the major challenges we face do exist and are within grasp, but they will require a great deal of innovation and dramatic changes in our economies and societies, as well as in the institutions, laws and rules that govern them. Our life habits and modes of consumption will also need to change drastically.

1.2. Social media and the age of fake news

Falsehoods, misinformation, disinformation and conspiracies have always existed, but today they are served and magnified by the dominance and reach of social media and the virality of fake news. Furthermore, the manner in which social media now structure the communication between individuals can affect the collective ability of certain groups to form reliable beliefs. This manifests in two ways. (1) We can opt, as we so often do on social media, only to interact with people who share our beliefs and refuse to do so with people who challenge them. In the process, by virtue of only connecting with those who think like us, we lose true connectivity and close down channels of vital communication. This creates partitions and polarization. (2) All sorts of influencers, be they government agencies, industry groups or even individuals, now have direct access to "ready-made" large groups of people with whom they can create a relation of trust and dependency, thus aggravating and even inflaming polarization. It should come as no surprise that research conducted during the pandemic has exposed a link between COVID-related uncertainty and anxiety and an increased likelihood of adhering to conspiracy theories.[4] This is part of the reason why powerful anti-science movements prolong the waning of the COVID-19 pandemic, hindering both public health and, more fundamentally, our ability to move forward in unison. Beyond the limits of the pandemic, the abundance of fake news and its ability to magnify and manipulate polarization hinders our ability to deal successfully with the momentous collective action problems that humanity faces.

In light of this, how can we best understand the necessity and relevance of the changes that are coming, the way we can influence their trajectory, and the role that systemic connectivity, social media and fake news play in all this? This is hard and there is no one simple answer. We must respond to questions like: What do we do next? What choices do we want to make? How can we fix what doesn't work? How can we put in place the corresponding new policies and solutions? How can we grasp the ideas that underpin them? How can we make these ideas palatable so that a large majority of citizens embrace them? The magnitude of the task is head-spinning! Its complexity far exceeds the cognitive capabilities of any single individual or the collective understanding of any single academic discipline and/or professional practice. The reason is straightforward: academics and other professionals tend to excel at thinking in a narrow field and to do so rely on a particular conceptual and methodological framework, leaving little or no time to connect with other disciplines or professions. This can and often does result in a shared disquiet of being both overwhelmed by the complexity of the task and having a limited understanding of its scope. Take the concatenation between economic, geopolitical, societal, technological and environmental issues as an example. Apart from the obvious cognitive limitations that an overload of information and rising complexity impose upon us, we are all restricted in our understanding of things by the boundaries of our professional lives. If we are an economist, we specialize in economics and find it hard to grasp what's happening in other fields, like geopolitics, technology or the environment. If we are an artificial intelligence (AI) specialist, we may find it difficult to comprehend what happens in the realm of social sciences and to understand the extent to which culture and social norms dictate how or if societies will "adopt" and adapt to new technologies. And so on. The point is this: we all tend to operate in our silos and often fail to connect the indispensable dots between disparate fields. Therefore, our response to new facts or situations and how we make sense of the world is over reliant on, and ultimately shaped by, how those people we know, or trust, are doing so. This fundamental process of exchanging, understanding and evaluation takes place via stories, or narratives.

1.3. The power of narratives

As the most effective of conduits for ideas, narratives have the unique power to help us determine what's going on, what lies ahead and what needs to be done, hence the title of this book. Defined in the simplest possible terms, a narrative is a story about something. More aptly for the purpose of *The Great Narrative*, it is also "a way of presenting or understanding a situation or series of events that reflects and promotes a particular point of view or set of values".[5] Some of the "narrators" we interviewed for this book go further, like John Hagel who draws a distinction between stories and narratives: "Stories are self-contained – they have a beginning, a middle and end (…). Narratives [are] open-ended. There is no resolution yet. There's some kind of big threat or opportunity out in the future and it's not yet clear whether it will be addressed. The resolution of the narrative hinges on you – the people being addressed by the narrative. Your choices and actions will help to determine how the narrative plays out."[6]

Stories are essential to us because as human beings and social animals, we are storytelling creatures. The philosopher Jean-Paul Sartre said it in *Nausea* (1938): "A man is always a teller of tales, he lives surrounded by his stories and the stories of others, he sees everything that happens to him through them; and he tries to live his life as if he were recounting it." Robert Shiller, the "father" of Narrative Economics, goes one step further, linking narratives to the decisions we make: "The human brain has always been highly tuned towards narratives, whether factual or not, to justify ongoing actions."[7] The rich scholarly literature about narratives makes it clear that we think, act and communicate in terms of narratives, and each interpretation, understanding or model of how the world operates begins with a story. Narratives provide the context in which the facts we observe can be interpreted, understood and acted upon. In that sense, they equate to much more than the stories we tell, write or illustrate figuratively; they end up being the truths, or the ideas we accept as truths, that underpin the perceptions that shape our "realities" and in the process form our cultures and societies. Through narratives, we explain how we see things, how these things work, how we make decisions and justify them, how we understand our place in the world and how we try to persuade others to embrace our beliefs and values.[8] To sum up: narratives shape our perceptions, which in turn form our realities and end up influencing our choices and actions. They are how we find meaning in life.

This book offers a constellation of interrelated narratives that shed light on what's coming and what to do about it. *The Great*

Narrative coalesces around one central story and derives from a collaborative effort with some of the world's leading thinkers to fashion longer-term perspectives and co-create a narrative that can help guide the creation of a more resilient, inclusive and sustainable vision for our collective future. It relies to a substantial extent, but not exclusively, on interviews conducted with 50 of the world's foremost global thinkers and opinion-makers who come from a broad spectrum of academic disciplines and from diverse geographies and backgrounds. Undoubtedly, thousands upon thousands of prominent academics, researchers, scientists, professors, foresight specialists and influential writers exist who could have made it to the list. There was, therefore, a degree of arbitrariness in deciding on the 50. We are confident, however, that the 50 we chose are "legitimate" in the sense that all of them will leave an imprint in their domain of expertise (and often beyond) and tend to be listened to by people outside their field. In short, their narratives are influential – they do matter. Whether or not we agree with them, these narratives titillate our imagination and entice us to flirt (even engage) with the ideas they present. This is critical. All too often, we tend to favour well-established ideas that are deeply interwoven with and influenced by our personal and professional lives. Put another way, we don't think "out of the box" nearly enough. As a result, we limit our exposure to those other ideas that can create an "Aha" or "Eureka" moment and compel us to think a bit differently, question some of our beliefs and assumptions, and make new mental connections. As you read this book, we hope you'll come to the realization that the 50 narratives can help us see the world differently and expand our mental map about what needs to be done to make it a better place. Each narrative does it from its own perspective and by the mere virtue of cognitive diversity. Each exposes us to other people's influential ideas. Drawn together, they create an interesting canvas – a great series of narratives in which we can engage to shape the society and the economy we want.

Exposing and discussing the ideas embedded in diverse narratives is what this book is all about. Moving them forward in the realms of decision-making and policy is also part of our endeavour. Actions, solutions and policies always begin with a "big" idea. Big ideas not only power our economies (they are the real engine of economic growth), but they also drive the world. When a big idea breaks through and becomes influential, it can turn into a viral narrative: it takes off and becomes contagious, making its way into policies as well as business and investors' decisions. Through the sheer work and imagination of those who originate them, ideas spur creativity and become the foundation of discovery, innovation and change. They can also become a call to action. If ideas were to be considered as an economic good, economists would call them in their jargon a "non-excludable" and "non-rival" good. Ideas are non-excludable because of their free nature: nobody can effectively be excluded from consuming (or generating) an idea. Ideas are also non-rival because they can be utilized by someone without reducing their availability to others: all can enjoy "consuming" an idea without preventing others from doing so. As the saying goes: "If I give you a dollar and you give me a dollar, each of us will only have one dollar. But if you give me one idea and I give you another idea, we will both have two ideas." This specific feature of ideas bestows them "with a natural property to generate aggregate nondecreasing returns to scale".[9] Put in plain language: the more the better, and the more ideas we have, the more they will generate! *The Great Narrative* offers a profusion of interesting and sometimes intriguing ideas mediated by the interviews we conducted with 50 global thinkers and opinion-makers.

This book is about ideas and how they may coalesce to form a Great Narrative. It is also, and most importantly, about how some of these ideas may or should make their way into policy- and decision-making. To reiterate: they go beyond the realm of theory and are a call to action. We adopt the view that, as they recover from the pandemic and embark on a path to radical and accelerated change, our societies and economies should be more inclusive and attuned to the needs of our global commons – and more resilient.

The Great Narrative is a hybrid between an essay, a manifesto and a light academic précis. It addresses such a large range of subjects that it is by necessity very synthetic (synthesis is a process of simplification but it goes without saying that being simple is not the same as being simplistic). Some ideas and narratives presented in the book may seem a bit out of the mainstream, but they are always supported and constrained by the factual evidence available in academic literature and in policy circles. *The Great*

Narrative is deliberately written with a minimum of academic jargon to make it palatable to the broadest possible readership. The text is accessible and easy to read but remains conceptually and methodologically robust. To interrupt its flow as little as possible, the multiple references to the academic and business literature appear at the end. *The Great Narrative* draws primarily from the interviews and conversations we had with our chosen 50 global thinkers and opinion-makers from June to November 2021. It is complemented by numerous other conversations we were privileged to have with leaders from business, government, civil society, as well as academia. In addition, it benefits from the input of a two-day brainstorming session hosted in November 2021 by the Government of the United Arab Emirates in Dubai with most of our 50 narrators and some of their peers (a most propitious place to elaborate a Great Narrative as, to our knowledge, the UAE is the only country in the world to have a "Ministry of Possibilities" aimed at building "new government systems for the future"). It is, in that sense, a community-sourced book, the product of the "enlightened wisdom" of a crowd's (the Forum community) vision. Direct attributions have been minimized, but all our interviewees are mentioned by name when we refer to their ideas or quote them verbatim. The list of the 50 contributors appears at the end of the book.

We would be thrilled if this book allows some of our readers to broaden their perspectives and if it even incites some of them to change their mind about a particular issue and helps them more meaningfully address it. Again, *The Great Narrative* is a call to action and a platform to move the agenda forward on some of the most critical issues that we collectively face.

The Great Narrative is structured in two main blocks. The first part is about problems. The second part is about solutions. The introduction sets the scene. The first part assesses the issues and challenges that we will collectively face in our post-pandemic era in five intertwined macro categories: economic, environmental, geopolitical, societal and technological. The second part looks at the solutions and the way forward from a multiplicity of perspectives – both individual and collective in nature. The conclusion investigates the way in which our mindsets and our sense of optimism, pessimism or pragmatism can help us (or otherwise) navigate the current maelstrom. The list of foremost global thinkers and opinion-makers and their titles are appended in the Annex.

2. Post-COVID Issues and Challenges

The world faces a maelstrom of global challenges. To cite some of the most major: unsustainable economic growth, geopolitical rivalries, environmental degradation, inequalities, pandemics and cybercrimes. The aim of these opening sections is to delineate and focus on the main issues using five different prisms that often interact with each other.

2.1. Conceptual framework

It is impossible to understand what is going on in the complex times that characterize today's world without a robust conceptual framework. To this end, we use the one developed by the Global Risks Network of the World Economic Forum, which divides global issues into five macro categories: economics, environment, geopolitics, society and technology.[10] This is a neat, simple and yet "all-encompassing" categorization of what's happening in the world. Any global issue of any significance necessarily belongs to one of these five key macro categories.

The following sections present them in a linear manner (one after the other) for reasons of convenience and simplicity but, as briefly stated in the introduction, interdependence and systemic connectivity define our world. Even though our brains incline us to think in linear terms and within the boundaries of an academic discipline, the world that surrounds us is non-linear and a mishmash of issues that don't fit neatly into any one silo. Our world is complex, adaptive, fast-paced and ambiguous and, as we argued in *The Great Reset*, it possesses quantum properties. We often think of it as if it were an emanation of the classical world of post-Newtonian physics – characterized by linearity, predictability and to some extent even determinism – but such a world doesn't exist. Today, possibly more than ever because of increased interdependence, it even exhibits certain properties of quantum physics: it is highly interconnected, uncertain and incredibly complex. The quantum metaphor (albeit just that) seems apt to describe such a world.

It is therefore limiting and conceptually wrong to think about one specific macro category without taking into consideration the way in which it intersects with the others. Thinking about economics without relating them to social issues, or about geopolitics without incorporating technology or, for that matter, thinking about any of the five macro categories in isolation from the four others, constitutes a dead end. The reason is straightforward: the five we've chosen as our conceptual framework are intricately interdependent. The risks and opportunities they harbour are fully interconnected. Each individual risk always conflates with the others and each has the potential to create ricochet effects by provoking further risks. To give an example, an extreme weather event (an environmental risk) can exacerbate food price inflation (an economic risk) that could in turn cause large-scale involuntary migration (a societal risk) and possibly trigger state collapse (a geopolitical risk). This shows the phenomenon of contagion by systemic connectivity. Similarly, an opportunity arising in one macro category (like the fast-paced acceleration of innovation and deployment of new technologies) can directly benefit another macro category through a specific and direct impact. Drone surveillance (something impossible until just a few years ago) to mitigate the risk of deforestation (a key environmental risk) offers such an example. Risks conflate, but so too do opportunities.

As observed in the introduction, the rapid and abrupt changes happening in our five macro categories are all occurring simultaneously and amplifying each other. This is most obvious with the environment. Environmental degradation and climate change are already having a profound impact on how our economies, societies and international relations (geopolitics) function. In turn, technology plays a critical role in how climate change is being addressed and some of its risks mitigated. The concatenation between these five macro categories means that we are in the midst of transitions on an epic scale. Every living generation thinks it is at the cusp of a "new era", but might it really be true this time? We don't know, but it is hard to deny that the world is changing faster than we may realize and that we are living through a period of profound transformations. It's a rare occurrence when our economies, our societies, geopolitics, the environment and tech can all be said to be changing concomitantly, rapidly and often abruptly, with second, third, fourth and more round-effects that affect them all. Our collective juries remain "out" on where all this will lead, principally because of two notions at the core of our conceptual framework: complexity and velocity.

2.1.1. Complexity

When researching this book and during our interviews, the word "complexity" emerged repeatedly, often alluded to in terms of how it makes it more difficult to comprehend what's going on in the world. In private conversations, we also heard decision-makers confess "they are a bit lost" or "don't really know what's happening". This is understandable: complexity creates limits to our knowledge and understanding of things. It might thus be that today's increasing complexity overwhelms the capabilities of decision-makers to make the most appropriate, sensible or well-informed decisions. Naturally, what is true for decision-makers is also true for the rest of us. Moisés Naím put it neatly when he said: "I've grown very attached to a statement made in the 1930s by José Ortega y Gasset, a famous Spanish philosopher and thinker, who said, "We do not know what is happening to us." And that's exactly what's happening to us. There are all kinds of tectonic changes, major societal changes, that we know are affecting us – climate change, for instance. It's going to touch our lives, families, work, employees, clients, colleagues, societies, communities – our lifestyle will change. But we don't know how we'll end up".[11] This is complexity at work. It baffles us.

Put in the simplest possible terms, complexity is "stuff we don't understand or find difficult to understand". In the words of the psychologist Herbert Simon, a complex system "is one made up of a large number of parts that interact in a non-simple way".[12] Complex systems are often characterized by an absence of visible causal links between their elements, which makes them impossible to predict. Intuitively, we grasp that the more complex a system is, the less is our ability to understand it[13] and to control it, and the greater the likelihood that something might go wrong and that a problem might occur and propagate.

Complexity can loosely be measured by three things: (1) the amount of information or the number of components in a system; (2) the interconnectedness, defined as the dynamic of reciprocal responsiveness – between these pieces of information or components; and (3) the effect of non-linearity (non-linear elements are often called "tipping points", discussed in greater detail in the context of climate change in section 2.3). Non-linearity is a key feature of complexity because it means that a change in just one component of a system can give rise to a surprising and disproportionate effect elsewhere. The words "black swans", "known unknowns" or "butterfly effects" epitomize non-linearity. It thus comes as no surprise that many narratives about today's world and how complex it is associate complexity with "surprises", "turbulence", "volatility" and "uncertainty".

In just a few decades, the amounts of information and interconnectedness have dramatically increased, rendering the systems in which we operate (our societies and economies, our systems of governance, our social contracts, our financial markets, our supply chains, and so on), more complex than in the past. They all are "complex adaptive systems", meaning that their properties are not set in stone and cannot be reduced to the elegant and predictive mathematical formalisms that apply to physical sciences like astronomy and physics. Systems in the living universe must be viewed instead as systems of interactions that are both complex and adaptive. Our societies, economies, our political systems and all our institutions represent a "cat's cradle" of interdependence and interconnections. They are adaptive in the sense that their behaviour is driven by interactions between human beings who respond to events and situations by adapting to changing conditions (and in so doing modify the initial conditions). Many models, particularly in economics, would have us believe that we do this in a rational manner that remains constant across time. Far from it! Our decisions are not always driven by our best interests and our "preferences" are far from being stable; they change all the time. The image of the *homo economicus* relentlessly pursuing his self-interest through the maximization of utility is a caricature. As humans, our conduct is also motivated by sentiments of empathy and generosity, and our decisions are often based on emotions, such as fear, surprise and happiness. Since the "behaviour" of such complex adaptive systems is driven by the interactions between nodes (the organizations, the institutions, the people – us!), they can become confused and "unruly" in times of stress. In short, complex adaptive systems are messy! They possess contradictory qualities in the sense that they can simultaneously be both robust and fragile. All adaptive networks exhibit a tipping-point property, which means that connections serve as a shock absorber but, beyond a certain critical stage, they become shock-amplifiers and problems cascade. Furthermore, feedback effects under stress amplify the fragility with great velocity. We saw that with big macro shocks as different as the Great Financial Crisis (with the fire-sales of assets after the collapse of Lehman Brothers in September 2008 and the subsequent hoarding of liquidity) and the pandemic (when the reproduction rate of the virus became such that it caused an exponential growth of incidence rates and brought almost everything to a halt). As a rule of thumb, the greater the complexity, the greater the uncertainty: complexity amplifies uncertainty because it becomes impossible to spot the weakest link in the chain.

The science of complex systems is interdisciplinary. By mixing mathematics, computer science, biology, physics, psychology, economics, ecology, epidemiology and other disciplines as well, it breaks down the artificial barriers that erect silos between academic professions. David Krakauer, a professor of Complex Systems and the President of the Santa Fe Institute, stated during our interview that a set of concepts help to understand why "the current world is one of complex causality". These concepts are relatively new and live in this constellation of concepts that we might call transmissibility, infectivity and cascades, among others, that are more familiar from the study of disease (which COVID-19 made clear to everyone). But there are others: tipping points, critical points, scaling phenomena, issues of collective intelligence, and the wisdom of crowds. Many ideas have emerged over the past few decades to help us make sense of the world, but they're very new. A constellation of concepts, growing out of complex systems, are very useful, but we don't know how they all connect. They point towards this more unified theory or synthetic understanding of complex reality.[14] In *The Great Narrative*, we refer often to such notions because they make the most sense in explaining what's going on now. Equally, they must be part of our conceptual framework because only they can explain the messiness or ambiguity of what's coming next. As the futurist Amy Zalman put it to us: "Humanity is entering a time that is chaotic and will be difficult to name, so it will actually be a period of multiple things, with perhaps utopias and dystopias unfolding in front of us."

2.1.2 Velocity

Everything is happening much faster than it used to, because technological advances and, to a lesser extent, globalization have created a culture of immediacy. We operate in a real-time society in which everything is needed and wanted right away. As a result, we constantly feel pressed for time and have the nagging feeling that the pace of life is ever increasing. This new culture of immediacy, obsessed with speed, seems to be in all aspects of our lives, from "just-in-time" supply chains (shaken-up by COVID) to "high-frequency" trading, from speed dating to fast food and fast delivery. It is so pervasive that some thinkers have called this new phenomenon the "dictatorship of urgency".[15] The broad result is that the shelf life of a product or an idea, the life cycle of a CEO or a project, are contracting sharply and often unpredictably. It also creates the impression that global events unfold at a furious pace, so furious that it can leave us cognitively stranded and incapable of making sense of what's happening. This sense of confusion is heightened by the constant "noise" to which we are all exposed. Comparable to the advent of the 24-hour news channels 40 years ago, now the myriad letters of information, the unceasing flow of news provided by social media and other digital outlets bombard us with an unending stream of alerts and notifications that often reduce rather than enhance our understanding. We have so much information and analyses that it's hard to know how to absorb it all in a meaningful manner. Not only does velocity take extreme forms, but it can also engender perverse effects. "Impatience" and unreasonable expectations, for example, affect the behaviour of many societal groups, ranging from participants in the financial markets obsessed with momentum trading (based on velocity) to voters who demand quasi-immediate results from the politicians they've elected, and consumers upset that the physical delivery of their digital order could take more than a few hours, as if a book or a dress or a vacuum-cleaner delivered in 12 hours rather than four were going to alter the meaning of life!

The fundamental reason that explains this astonishing rise in velocity is undoubtedly tech and digital connectivity. More than

60% of the world's population is now online, compared to 42% in 2015 and less than 8% just 20 years ago. At the end of 2021, more than 80% of the world's total population had a smart phone. A total of 57% of the world's population is active on social media, a ratio that rises to over 80% in northern America. Other explanations for the rise in velocity point to the "scarcity" element: as societies get richer, time becomes more valuable and is therefore perceived as ever scarcer. This is proven by studies showing that people in wealthy cities always walk faster than in poor cities and that, in general, rich people tend to walk faster than poor people. No matter what the causal explanation is, the endgame of all this is obvious: we are all being subjected to constant, but discontinuous, rapid change. Velocity is everywhere, whether it's crises, social discontent, technology, geopolitical upheaval, the financial markets or shocks like the pandemic; everything now runs on fast-forward and tends to take us by surprise. This was manifest at the end of 2021. In retrospect, some the most significant macro events that took place at that time surprised us: whether it was the suddenness of supply shock disruptions, the return of inflation, the advent of a global energy crisis, the abruptness of certain policy measures taken by Chinese President Xi Jinping against tech, or the resurgence of COVID-19 in Europe. They all happened faster than most analysts and the public had anticipated. Often, exponential growth is the reason behind this apparent extreme velocity. We often (and wrongly) equate exponential growth with fast growth, but it's different. Fast means high speed while exponential growth is rather about the way in which speed keeps evolving. In simple terms, there is exponential growth when there is a fixed doubling of time, thus it shows greater increases as time goes by. Pandemics tend to follow this pattern (they can progress at breakneck speed, with a rate of infection doubling in just a few days, as COVID-19 did in March 2020). At the moment, the same applies to technological advance.[16] Exponential growth is hard to grasp. It is in fact so baffling to our cognitive functions that we often deal with it by developing exponential "myopia",[17] thinking of it as nothing more than "very fast". But in a famous experiment conducted in 1975, two psychologists found that, when asked to predict an exponential process, we often underestimate it by a factor of 10.[18] It's no surprise that we get overtaken by events! Naím observed in our conversation with him that, "We are getting the trends correctly, but we are constantly being proven wrong on the velocity. We know what the changes that will alter the world are, but we underestimate, and have a long history of underestimating, velocity."

An important and far-reaching consequence of velocity is the following: leaders and decision-makers have more information and more analysis than ever before, but less time to decide. In addition, velocity has created a problem of a-synchronicity between different groups whose time horizon differs. Of necessity, policy-makers and business leaders take time to decide, obliged as they are to consider different constituency groups and different interests. By contrast, non-state and non-corporate actors, like civil society, activists, traders or the electorate, react almost immediately to everything that happens (or doesn't happen).

The difference in tempos can be startling. It is particularly problematic in liberal democracies as they are subject to the vagaries of the electoral cycle. Worldwide, and more generally, we now expect everything to accelerate but also to improve. This produces burnout, a sense of estrangement and a nagging feeling of uneasiness or discomfort.

2.2. Economics

In 2020 and much of 2021, government policy alone stood between the global economy and the abyss. The pandemic upended the economic orthodoxy that had prevailed for decades, prompting policy-makers to abandoned austerity and spend their way out of the pandemic. All the nations that could afford to do so engaged in a "whatever-it-takes moment for large-scale, outside-the-box fiscal and monetary policies".[19] In rich countries, the governments and central banks' decision to pursue extraordinarily accommodative fiscal and monetary policies has proved effective, further fostered by successful vaccination campaigns (a reminder that economics and epidemiology cannot be separated).[20] Despite the dramatic global drop in GDP in 2020, all OECD countries should have recovered the lost ground by 2022. In developing countries and most emerging markets, the story is a very different one and the situation couldn't be starker. Their monetary and fiscal support was much more limited, if not non-existent, since they enjoy very little latitude to implement expansionary policies for risk of hammering their currencies and generating inflation; added to that, they have had limited access to vaccines. The damage inflicted by the pandemic will therefore be more profound and will last longer in the developing world. Globally, the recovery comes at the expense of sharply deteriorating debt-to-GDP ratios and huge question marks about the future of growth and debt crises. Thus, it will be protracted, uneven and uncertain.

2.2.1. Growth

Economic growth matters, both as a benchmark to measure success and the role it can play as an engine of human progress. In principle, the more a country grows, the better it can harness its full economic, social and human potential. Therefore, heads of government, public officials and politicians are under constant pressure to generate and report higher, faster growth.

At the time of writing at the end of 2021, growth in advanced economies is rebounding, much less so in most emerging markets and developing countries. When recovery from the pandemic will have played out and the vigour of the rebound exhausted its effect, global growth will likely return to the lukewarm levels it experienced prior to 2020. In the foreseeable future, the global economy will grow less than it did in the past for several secular reasons. They include, in no particular order: global ageing, inequalities,[21] a partial retreat from globalization and the supply risks it entails, high levels of indebtedness, geopolitical turmoil and Chinese growth's inevitable deceleration. Each of these factors, which often intersect with each other and amplify their effects, will constrain future economic growth.

But what sort of growth are we measuring and what sort of growth do we want? The pandemic and the great financial crisis (2008-2009) that preceded it have made it clear that GDP is an inadequate measure of progress. It is supposed to measure our common prosperity and global economic ascendency, but there is now quasi-universal recognition that it does not capture what matters most: climate action, sustainability, inclusivity, global cooperation, health and well-being. While economists and policy-makers acknowledge that nations need economic growth to recover from the pandemic, they also want to ensure that this growth is of a quality compatible with human, societal and environmental well-being. Therefore, they want an instrument that measures how nature is affected by our decision to produce and consume, that includes important (but not financially remunerated) contributions to society like childcare and volunteering, or that takes into consideration how profits are distributed. GDP measurement takes none of the aforementioned into account. The move to replace or supplement GDP with a better measure of human progress goes back to Simon Kuznets, the economist who conceived GDP shortly before World War II while immediately recognizing that his creation did not account for society's well-being. As Robert Kennedy said a few decades later: GDP measures everything "except that which makes life worthwhile", including the health, education and welfare of children.[22] The search to propose alternatives to GDP has been going on ever since. It includes, among others, Bhutan's "gross national happiness", Malaysia's "quality of life index", the "genuine progress indicator", the "better life index"[23] endorsed by the OECD, and the One-Earth balance sheet project.[24] All aim to complement or even replace GDP with social and/or environmental factors, but propose different methodologies to do so. While the quest continues, using GDP per capita (i.e. per person) instead of total GDP may be best. GDP per capita captures a crucial phenomenon ignored by most alternatives: the population decline faced by some countries. Japan proves the point. Most narratives depict it as a hopeless case of a nation that combines population decline and no growth, but when the data is adjusted for demographics and total GDP converted into GDP per capita, Japan does better than most. Its GDP per capita is high and growing and, since 2007, its real GDP per member of the working age population (a still narrower definition than per capita) has tended to rise faster than in any other G7 country. As the world ages and a rising number of countries experience net negative population growth, GDP per capita will be the best metric: it can rise even in a recession if the population shrinks more than total GDP, offering a less alarming picture than would otherwise be the case. The arguments for choosing per capita GDP include that it tends to correlate with measures that are strong predictors of life satisfaction (happiness), such as higher life expectancy, better social safety nets, lower infant mortality and poverty levels, less air pollution and corruption. This is borne out by the annual *World Happiness Report*[25] whose latest edition ranks just one country with a GDP per capita under $15,000 (Costa Rica) among the top 25 and none with a GDP per capita over $15,000 in the bottom 60.

In the coming years, no matter what happens with potential substitutes, many leaders will persist in their obsession with GDP growth maximization and therefore GDP will continue to underpin most decisions made in economic policy. However, as the world inevitably moves in a direction that uses a different lens to measure progress and becomes more conscious of the need to preserve what GDP doesn't measure (like biodiversity and social cohesion), we may take the view, at least in rich countries, that living with a few basis points of lower GDP growth doesn't amount to a catastrophe, particularly in countries that score well on environmental and social performance indicators (i.e. whose growth is "balanced" and of quality). We might even find we can live with such a scenario quite happily! This is not a rhetorical question. Consider the following: would you prefer to live in a country that ranks consistently among the highest in terms of subjective well-being (happiness) and abides by stringent environmental standards with unimpressive but decent rates of GDP growth, or in a country that grows at an average of 1 or 2 percentage points higher, but scores lower in environmental and social terms? Would you prefer a 2% growth rate in a pristine and socially stable environment or 4% in a heavily polluted place with little social cohesion? At one extreme, Japan's high living standards and elevated well-being indicators offer a salutary lesson that there is hope even in a quasi-absence of total GDP growth (but decent GDP per capita growth). In our conversation, Shu Yamaguchi called this situation "the completion of civilization", adding, "I wish to call it a 'plateau society', not a 'climbing society'. Japan in the 20th century was a climbing society, climbing the mountains and catching up with the United States and the United Kingdom. It worked very well but doesn't anymore. This is not stagnation, but a completion of modernization."[26] This argument is reflected in the consumption habits of some affluent consumers. They may express a desire to replace conspicuous consumption and material accumulation with new markers of distinction, like experiences instead of physical goods. They range from concerts to culinary experiments or visits to remote destinations (often with a purpose) and are found in services (the "non-tradable" sector) in which it's much harder to improve productivity.[27] This entails less GDP growth but could be seen as a sign of social progress.

The situation is very different in poor countries (and developing countries in general) where GDP growth will continue to matter considerably. Dambisa Moyo pointed this out when affirming that:

> We should be very worried about policies that (inadvertently) prejudice people in poor countries. I could be wrong, but I suspect people who say we could reduce our living standards are people who are already wealthy. If you have no access to energy, no access to healthcare or education, the prospects for the next generation are pretty poor, which is true for emerging markets where 90% of the world's population lives. The growth proposition is still highly attractive, which is why China obviously becomes a big player in this story.[28]

2.2.2. Public indebtedness

The last four decades saw the largest, fastest and most broad-based increase in total debt levels around the world. In 2021, it tripled to 350% of GDP, with public debt alone reaching almost 100% of GDP – a rise much amplified by the pandemic. Since COVID-19 began its onslaught, governments around the world have disbursed $17 trillion (the equivalent of 16% of global GDP) on fiscal support while central banks expanded their balance sheets by an aggregate of almost $8 trillion. It is hard, if not impossible, to tell at which precise level government debt becomes problematic. Recent policies suggest that the critical question is not "how much" but "what for". Obviously, public debt incurred to prevent a collapse of our economies and societies is distinct from that incurred to fund an unproductive policy agenda. It may be for this reason that much higher levels of public indebtedness than in the past are now being tolerated with markets seeming unconcerned (for the moment). Government debt cannot expand indefinitely without causing major problems and, in the end (that is, in the very long term), it must be dealt with via: (1) higher growth; (2) higher inflation; or (3) default. Debt monetization – an emergency option – will only go so far. Barring higher productivity (a possibility considered below), higher growth of sufficient magnitude is not a given, for all the reasons just mentioned. If robust long-term higher growth fails to materialize, a toxic mix of low growth and elevated inflation could arise. This risk of a scenario involving inflation and default occurring is at its greatest in emerging markets and developing economies.[29]

Inflation (or rather its absence) played a key role in the build-up of public debt. Its disappearance for many years meant that central banks not only tolerated rising budget deficits but facilitated them. As governments boosted spending without a concomitant increase in taxes, they issued bonds to finance the resulting deficit. In turn, central banks bought these bonds from investors as part of the quantitative easing programmes. By doing so, they decreased the interest rates at which governments borrow. As stated by Sebastian Mallaby in "The Age of Magic Money", "A finance ministry that sells debt to its national central bank is, roughly speaking, borrowing from itself. Just as central bankers are blurring the line between monetary policy and budgetary policy, so, too, are budgetary authorities acquiring some of the alchemical power of central bankers."[30]

The fact that global public debt is now at a post-World War II peak while central bank balance sheets in the past only reached similar heights at times of war makes the normalization of fiscal and monetary policies difficult, creating "daunting challenges for policymakers",[31] particularly so at a time of resurgent inflation. When interest rates will start increasing, the sustainability of the debt will be immediately at risk: debt servicing costs for governments could then rise dramatically.

****

What does this world of lower growth and higher debt portend? Among the plethora of effects, four stand out: (1) the end of convergence; (2) the resurgence of inflation; (3) the possible re-emergence of productivity; and (4) the strong emergence of crypto. The first two are of great concern. The third is a reason for hope. The fourth illustrates the major unknowns and uncertainties we must contend with.

(1) The end of convergence between rich and poorer countries might be provisional or become a systemic feature of the post-pandemic economic landscape. Currently, what looks certain is that the world economic recovery from the pandemic will be uneven. Prospects for most emerging and developing countries look far worse than those of the most developed ones – a divergence that will result in a two-speed global economy. International institutions like the International Monetary Fund (IMF) estimate that output in the rich world should return to its pre-pandemic level by 2022, and then rise slightly above it, while it will remain well below trend in the rest of the world until at least 2025. Two key reasons explain this disconnect: (1) the vaccination divides; and (2) differences in fiscal and monetary support. Regarding the first, in October 2021, almost 60% of people in the rich world were fully vaccinated against COVID-19, compared with only 36% in emerging economies and barely 5% in the poorest countries. This means that life can start returning to "normal" only in the rich world. Regarding the second, most emerging markets and almost the totality of developing countries had no or little fiscal space to react to the negative shock inflicted by the pandemic. When some decided to launch expansionary fiscal policies nonethe-

less, capital outflows ensued, hammering their exchange rate and fuelling inflation. Worse, they had difficulties in maintaining their existing levels of debt because their creditors refused to roll over their loans in fear of a worsening crisis. In the early months of the pandemic, more than 90 countries petitioned the IMF for assistance. Moving forward and in addition, when the policy tightening takes place in the US, it will most likely cause large capital outflows from emerging markets, and a subsequent increase in capital costs. Knock-on effects are almost inevitable: troubles in the developing world will affect rich countries. The greater the divergence (instead of convergence), the greater the risk of financial instability caused by contagion effects, and of surges in uncontrolled migration and geopolitical turmoil.

(2) Most analysts and policy-makers did not anticipate the resurgence of inflation in the third quarter of 2021. The global economy rebounded from last year's recession in a very strong manner (the strongest in 80 years), but that came with an equally fast rebound in global inflation. Initially, a majority of policy-makers and analysts, and the markets at large, thought that this resurgence would prove transient – a consequence of the robust demand triggered by the recovery and the resulting inability of supply chains to rapidly adjust. Monetary policy is ill-suited to respond to supply-shock generated by inflation, so central banks decided to "wait and see". The spike in inflation then proved to be both greater and longer-lived than initially expected. If evidence of wage

pressure materializes in high-income countries (it may well do so by the time this book is published), this could generate a wage-price spiral – the "nightmare" of central bankers. At the time of finalizing this manuscript in mid-December 2021, inflationary pressures are building up around the world. As a result, several systemically important countries like the United States and many emerging countries don't have much space (if any) to keep monetary policy loose and interest rates at very low levels. On 15 December 2021, Jerome Powell, the chairman of the Federal Reserve, said as much when he announced that the Fed would take a much more aggressive approach to taming resurgent inflation. If the pandemic lasts longer, creating further supply disruptions that in turn fuel inflationary pressures, the risk of stagflation (low growth combined with significant inflation) could become a real concern, endangering the recovery.

(3) The last 15 years have been characterized by the so-called "productivity paradox": despite the apparent progress in technology, productivity levels remained flat or, in some cases, even regressed, in advanced economies. "But a productivity boom is coming", asserts Stanford University professor Erik Brynjolfsson.[32] If it does happen, the re-emergence of productivity would be excellent news for economic growth. As the economist Paul Krugman once famously said: "Productivity isn't everything, but, in the long run, it is almost everything. A country's ability to improve its standard of living over time depends almost

entirely on its ability to raise its output per worker."[33] "Thanks" to the pandemic, it seems that productivity has, at last, been ignited. In the US, Europe and Japan, data points to an increase in total factor productivity growth – the most common way to measure productivity which consists essentially in doing more with less – of more than 2%. The most likely explanation consists in the ready acceptance of tech and the increased adoption of digital and automation technologies during the pandemic. The labour shortages that took place in the second half of 2021 should not only sustain productivity growth but could even spur it further by forcing companies to innovate more. Since levels of economic growth equate to changes in productivity and changes in the labour force, a possible upsurge in productivity would be excellent news for economic growth, even more so at a time when the labour force is declining in much of the world.

(4) The strong and rapid emergence of cryptocurrencies, and more broadly fintech, entangles economics with technological innovation in such a complex way that it makes it hard to identify how the causality runs and what some of the potential applications and policy implications might be. Analysts and media reports give the impression that national currencies already compete with cryptocurrencies since individuals and institutions can hold digital wallets with whichever crypto asset they chose. As Parag Khanna states:

> We are about to enter an age of global monetary competition, where national currencies must earn their place in someone's wallet portfolio every hour of every day, even among citizens of their own countries. The digital version of the Japanese yen will be plunged into head-to-head global competition with the Swiss franc, the Brazilian real, and any other asset with an open capital account, including Bitcoin. Everyone becomes a foreign-exchange trader, all the time, and only the best national currencies – or cryptocurrencies – are ever held by anyone.[34]

It might be that government-supported cryptocurrencies compete with each other, as hinted at by Khanna. If they do so, they'd blur the line with fiat money and would change the financial system in terms of financial stability and traditional monetary policy in a way that nobody can yet predict.

Currently, both monetary authorities and private institutions issue cryptocurrencies as viable, mainstream payment vehicles. Central banks and governments experiment with "govcoins", or Central Bank Digital Currencies, while private "sponsors" develop "stablecoins" – cryptocurrencies whose value is pegged to the value of an underlying asset. The trajectory and endgame for govcoins and stablecoins remain unknown, but their respective fates may ultimately be decided by adoption and above all regulation (the power of the state). The only certainty:

their economic, societal and possibly geopolitical impacts will be considerable. Will physical cash still be accepted? Will cryptocurrencies pervade our privacy? How will they redefine the role of technology in our daily lives? What will their impact be on the effectiveness of monetary policy? Could they foster greater financial inclusion? Could cryptocurrencies advance environmental objectives and the policies that support them? Could they be used to accelerate the demise of the US dollar? Will they become an instrument of geopolitical dominance? These are just some of the questions for which we do not yet have any clear response.
The intermingling of economic, environmental, geopolitical, societal and technological issues is constantly expanding the universe of what we neither know nor understand. In addition, the velocity of this ever-evolving change further constrains our comprehension, and thus the capacity of the policy responses to meet the challenges they raise. Disruption is coming. It will be both good and bad, and major.

2.3. Environment

Our current apparent inability to end the critical environmental and climate crisis (they are one and the same as nature and climate are inextricably linked) or to at least keep it under control, is the greatest collective action problem we've ever been confronted with.[35] Humanity has never faced an endeavour more complex, ambitious and far-reaching than arresting the collapse of our ecosystem and stabilizing the climate.

2.3.1. The facts and the science

We've known about global warming for more than 50 years. Some industries have understood the risk for decades but chose to say nothing, while some experts from the scientific community and a few pundits started warning publicly about it in the 1970s. A few milestones show that the international community was aware of the risk posed by climate change and was willing to address it as early as 30 years ago.[36] In 1992, more than 130 nations signed the UN Convention on Climate Change at the Rio Earth Summit. In 1997, in Kyoto, 36 rich countries set reduction targets. In 2015, the signatories to the Paris Agreement agreed to limit the increase in global warming to below 2°C. All this for (almost) naught. As an authoritative UN report put it in October 2021: "Climate action so far has been characterized by weak promises, not yet delivered."[37] Sadly, the outcome of COP26 does little to reverse this judgement. The positive steps that transpired are welcomed, but they are not commensurate with the immensity of the challenge.

According to the *UN Emissions Gap Report*, we are still falling short of our collective commitment to reduce carbon emissions. Current national pledges (as of late October 2021, just before COP26) only take 7.5% off of predicted 2030 emissions. This is totally inadequate. To reach the Paris Agreement's goal to limit warming to 1.5–2°C, far more ambitious pledges are necessary. As the UN report states, reductions of 30% are needed by 2030 to stay on the least-cost pathway for 2°C and of 55% reductions for 1.5°C. The scientists who wrote the report estimate that if nations only implement their unconditional nationally determined contributions (NDCs)[38] as they stand, we'll most likely hit global warming of around 2.7°C by the end of this century. The UN's new assessment made during COP26 to account for the commitments and pledges made in Glasgow doesn't alter that projection. Nor does a report published by Climate Action Tracker shortly after COP26.[39] Franz Timmermans, the EU commissioner summed it up: "The honest truth is we are not where we need to be, not even close."[40] It is possible that additional net-zero pledges like those made by firms on environmental, social and corporate governance (ESG) efforts could cut another 0.5°C off global warming, but they are ambiguous, often based on dubious data and science, often delayed, not always folded into the NDCs and almost always non-binding. In the words of Tariq Fancy, a former BlackRock chief investment officer for sustainable investing, they'll have a "negligible impact"[41] in addressing the greatest market failure in history. The situation is changing very quickly, and the financial industry may hopefully invalidate this forecast, but an overwhelming number of scientists concur with the grim assessment of a 2.7°C increase by the end of this century. Some go further: a recent survey conducted by *Nature*[42] reveals that many authors of the Intergovernmental Panel on Climate Change (IPCC) report expect the world to warm by at least 3°C by the end of the century. They also expect to see the catastrophic effects of climate change in their lifetimes.

In short, experts and scientists have never been clearer in analysing and assessing the existential threat facing humanity. "It is unequivocal": these are the first three words of the sixth and most recent IPCC report:[43] "It is unequivocal that human influence has warmed the atmosphere, ocean and land. Widespread and rapid changes in the atmosphere, ocean, cryosphere and biosphere have occurred." By now, climate change is apparent for all of us to see and feel. Outbreaks of extreme weather events are occurring everywhere (progressively becoming the norm) as are weather disasters like once-in-a-thousand-year floods, giant wildfires, deadly heat waves and powerful hurricanes. The data makes this plain. The World Meteorological Organization recently reported that the number of climate change induced disasters has increased by 500% in the last 50 years, resulting in $3.64 trillion worth of damage and the loss of 2 million lives, disproportionately impacting the poorer countries.[44] There is little doubt in the scientific community that this is only the beginning and that climate change will get worse in the years ahead. We all stand on the brink of not just abrupt and violent change, but disaster, as we've reached the point of no return.

In our conversation with him, Johan Rockström developed a "grand narrative" worth quoting at length because it highlights in a magistral manner the magnitude and the urgency of the problem, as well as the significance of what "no return" means:

> When you put all the evidence on the table from all the lines of science, one has to unfortunately

accept that we must now explore the following question: Are we at risk of destabilizing the entire planet? That is, are we at risk of undermining the life-support system that we depend on, and are we at risk of pushing the planet away from the extraordinarily stable state it's been in since we left the last Ice Age, and which has been the state of the planet that has enabled civilizations to develop? My focus is on defining a safe operating space for humanity on a stable and resilient planet. That's the grand narrative: we now, in the depths of the Anthropocene where humanity is the dominating force of change, must reconnect to the planet, must become stewards to the planet, and must recognize that the planet has boundaries that are non-negotiable. The big new future for humanity is to be successful, equitable and profitable, all the desirable attributes within the safe operating space of a stable planet. That's the big challenge: to return and have a safe landing on Earth. (…) We do face an existential crisis – not that we're at risk of collapsing tomorrow, but the biggest risk is that we've entered the decisive decade for humanity's future on Earth. That's a very dramatic statement, an existential statement. Does that mean we'll fall over an escarpment on January 1, 2031, if we fail? No. What's at stake is that we're very close to the points of no return, at risk of crossing thresholds and pressing on buttons of irreversible changes, meaning the planet would not fall over an escarpment, but would irreversibly start drifting away to a state that would no longer be able to support the modern world as we know it. Perhaps it will take 100, 200 or 300 years before we sit there with 40% of the land area on Earth being uninhabitable, sit there with a 10-metre sea-level rise, and sit there with extreme weather events, fires, and disease. The full impact of that may be a painful journey over a long time but the key is, as far as we know now from science, that we determine in the next decade what path we choose: whether we commit all future generations to this negative pathway, an existential undermining, or whether we veer off towards a new future, which is where we land the world on a stable planet. That's the drama. That's why I talk about a planetary emergency. An emergency is when you face a catastrophic risk, but just because you face such a risk doesn't necessarily make it an emergency. It's an emergency when a catastrophic risk is multiplied by a lack of time. Science has been warning for decades that we have catastrophic risks, but now we're also running out of time. The global carbon budget is eaten up; there's no more ocean or atmosphere we can exploit; the rainforests are disappearing, and

> there's no more temperate forest to rely on. We cannot push the system further. We've reached a saturation point. So, when you multiply catastrophic risk with a low time window [it] equals emergency. That's why you go out with a fire brigade to extinguish a fire in your house, because you're in a time-desperate situation. We've been showing scientifically for a very long time that 2020 is the last chance of bending the global curve of emissions. That's been in the fourth and fifth assessments of the IPCC, but have we bent the curve? No. We've passed 2020, and we've entered the decisive decade. We need to cut emissions in half, we must halt biodiversity loss, and we need an end to this unsustainable path. That's what makes it existential.

This is a dramatic statement, both literally and metaphorically, which comes from one of the most authoritative scientists in the field. To comprehend how climate change will evolve, it is essential to refer to the critical difference between a "saturation point" and a "tipping point". The former means that we have reached the point of planetary boundaries regarding the global average atmospheric carbon dioxide level, as the science tells us that when we exceed 350 parts per million (we are currently at 415 parts per million), we enter the saturation point for the atmosphere. This indicates that, "We've filled up the entire capacity of the Earth's system to absorb the stress and the pressures caused by humans without causing impacts (…). We've loaded so much pressure, we've cut down and exploited so much, that the planet can't take it anymore."[45] The latter, by contrast, is something scientifically defined. A tipping point is an exact point, the threshold beyond which significant and often unstoppable change takes place. A system benefits from multiple stable states, separated by thresholds that can be crossed by a shift in feedbacks. A healthy rainforest system, for example, could flip over to become a savannah if, due to deforestation, it crosses the tipping point at which its tree mass can no longer sustain its water-recycling ecosystem. Similarly, a stable ice sheet (or glacier) in the mountains could flip over and irreversibly melt to become a lake. Ice sheets benefit from good feedback by being white (white surfaces reflect incoming heat and stay cool), "but once they start melting, they get darker, and at a certain point – a very specific point – they cross the threshold, the feedback shifts direction and they become self-warming because they become darker, and that's a tipping point". As Rockström has observed, we know about tipping points but we don't know exactly where the threshold lies. However, we do have evidence that we are either fast approaching some tipping points or have already crossed a few of them. "The West Antarctic ice shelf is already past the tipping point, as are the Arctic summer ice and tropical coral reefs (…). The big danger now is AMOC [Atlantic Meridional Overturning Circulation], the overturning of heat in the North Atlantic, along with the Amazon rainforest, the whole permafrost systems of the tundra in Siberia, the big temperate forests and the bark beetle outbreaks, and the question of whether we'll have stability across Greenland very much longer."

2.3.2. What needs to be done

Experts and scientists know what needs to be done to curb climate change or, at least, how to attenuate its progression and avert the risk that more tipping points will occur. For climate scientists, it boils down to reducing our greenhouse gas emissions (GHGs) as much and as fast as possible. Carbon sequestration will also be necessary. To meet the Paris Agreement objective of limiting global warming to below 2°C and ideally to 1.5°C, they estimate that in addition to the NDCs undertaken by over 120 countries mentioned earlier, a further 17-20 Gt of CO2 reductions and a 40% reduction in methane emissions would be required.[46] In addition, the IPCC calculated that we need to remove 100 billion to 1 trillion tonnes of CO2 by the end of the century.[47] But economics is the stumbling block. At this juncture, for reasons explained below, it is currently incredibly difficult to put into place policies aimed at delivering such ambitious targets. The (beleaguered) hope is that this will become easier as the climate crises intensifies, putting humanity against the wall and giving decision-makers no choice but to act in a radical manner.

The fundamental reasons that explain the paltry progress so far are threefold: (1) a lack of price for carbon emissions; (2) a relative ineffectiveness in promoting low-carbon technologies; and (3) the malfunctioning architecture of international climate accords.[48]

(1) There will never be real incentive to decarbonize without a price being put on carbon dioxide emissions around the world. Without it, governments, companies and consumers will simply not change their behaviour in volume and on a scale that matters. Currently, the global price of carbon emissions is almost zero (the World Bank estimated it at about $2 per tonne in 2019 and the IMF estimates it at $3 today). Carbon pricing plans exist in various places (the largest being the European Union Emissions Trading System), but they all have defects. They either set a relatively high price but one that only covers a fraction of their economies (less than half, in the case of the EU) or have a very high coverage rate but very low tax (such as the California cap and trade system). To be effective, a carbon price needs to be equal across countries and sectors, and high enough to have a meaningful effect. William Nordhaus estimates that to attain either the two-degree objective or the target of zero net emissions by 2050, carbon prices would have to rise to $300-500 per tonne by 2030, and go as high as $1,000 per tonne by 2050. He notes that these estimates are based on models that vary widely because the technologies needed to reach zero emissions are still in the making and therefore speculative. However, the prices estimated are considerably higher (by a factor of hundreds) than they are today.

(2) The inadequate investment in low-carbon technologies is caused by what Nordhaus calls "misaligned innovation incentives". Because fossil fuels still account for more than 80% of the world's primary energy consumption, it will take several hundred trillion in new capital to reach net-zero emissions over the next four decades (from $100 trillion to $300 trillion according to a rough estimate).[49] This won't happen unless governments massively increase their support for low-carbon technologies worldwide. The reasons are twofold: (1) The move to a zero-carbon global economy will necessitate the replacement of most parts of the energy infrastructure; (2) This in turn will require the development of new carbon-removal technologies that don't (or barely) exist today. Such development can only occur with strong government support because, as Nordhaus explains, "R&D suffers from a severe externality in the same way that climate change does", as public returns on green innovation are much larger than the private returns. The reason is the following: as economic returns rapidly spill over to other firms and future consumers, green inventors and entrepreneurs only receive a small fraction of the returns on their innovations (as already manifest with investments in carbon capture and sequestration). Then, the low prices of emissions (so dramatically under-priced) exacerbate the problem. It is therefore left to governments and public authorities to develop new low-carbon technologies and new energy sources (like hydrogen or fusion power), a situation that will persist until carbon emissions cease to be ridiculously under-priced.

The governments' priorities must also be rebalanced to correctly account for the threat posed by the climate emergency. Nordhaus points out that the US Government spent $60 billion in 2019 in R&D on military systems but 30 times less ($2 billion) in R&D on advanced energy and renewables. He posits that, "There may be a political logic to this disparity, [but] there is no societal logic to the imbalance given the climate threats the world faces in the coming years."

(3) The architecture of international climate accords and, more generally, the structure of international policy about climate change is beset by the problem of free-riding, the situation when someone (an individual, a company or a country) lacks the incentive to contribute voluntarily to the provision of a public good (in this case a liveable planet) but nonetheless benefits from it. In short, free-riders think along the lines of "let the others do the hard work and pay for it". Free-riding is a key reason why the world has made so little progress over the last 30 years in combating climate change. Many countries expect other countries to act first (perhaps for "legitimate" reasons as discussed below), waiting for them to do the "heavy lifting", which dramatically undermines the decisions and non-committal pledges made on the occasion of international agreements. The standard economic response to the free-rider problem can take two forms: (1) coercion through taxation and regulation; or (2) the appeal to the free-rider's altruistic sentiments and sense of social purpose. Neither of these two hypothetical solutions can work for

> climate change. The fundamental flaw of the international agreements, like the Kyoto Protocol or the Paris Agreement, is that they lack a binding international agreement. All the commitments and pledges made at each of the 26 UN conferences (and elsewhere) are "soft" and often even lack the actual policy mechanisms required for implementing them. Since the international community started to engage on climate change, no penalties of any kind have been imposed for non-participation, breaking a promise or commitment, or even withdrawing from an agreement (as in the case of the US and the Kyoto Protocol). This allows for and encourages free-riding on a massive scale. As for altruism, countries tend to privilege their national interests over global interests, thus neglecting to do their part when dealing with global issues, leading to outcomes that leave everybody worse off. This is particularly notable in the fight against climate change.

A comprehensive international climate policy must address these three mutually interdependent failures by putting into place a universal carbon pricing mechanism, a robust system for public support of low-carbon technologies, and a new architecture for international climate agreements. Most experts and market participants agree that no real progress will happen without systemic and even "aggressive" reforms that only governments have the ability, capacity and legitimacy to pursue. As an example, investing responsibly according to ESG criteria "will remain a fiction"[50] until an effective global carbon tax is imposed, consistent ESG standards are implemented, and a set of broad-based regulations penalize bad behaviour. But despite the necessity to avoid brutal capital shifts, time is of the essence. While waiting for this to happen, what other measures can be put in place?

Just before COP26, the Energy Transitions Commission, a global coalition of leaders from across the energy landscape, committed to achieving net-zero emissions by mid-century and enumerated six specific sets of action which, if agreed at the conference and implemented during the rest of the 2020s, could make it possible to achieve the 1.5°C target. All six are technically feasible and could be moved forward by governments and/or companies without the need for comprehensive internationally negotiated agreements. They are:[51]

(1) A significant and rapid reduction in methane emissions.
(2) The halting of deforestation and the beginning of reforestation.
(3) The decarbonization of the power sector and the acceleration of the phaseout of coal.
(4) The acceleration of the electrification of road transport.
(5) The acceleration of supply decarbonization in buildings, heavy industry and heavy transport.
(6) The reinvigoration of energy and resource efficiency.

With respect to these actions, the outcome of COP26 is mixed – at best. Some positive steps were taken, most notably pledges to reduce methane emissions and deforestation but, overall, they fall short of what is required to address in earnest our climate emergency. The promises made are neither binding nor yet accompanied by any concrete action plan. As for the more active involvement of the private sector towards net-zero objectives by 2050 (a pool of over $130 trillion of capital has been made available by the Glasgow Financial Alliance for Net Zero[52] (GFANZ) to transform the economy to net zero), it can only operate at scale with international carbon pricing, the elimination of fossil-fuel subsidies and mandatory climate-related financial disclosure. None of these looks likely to happen immediately in the absence of the policies and regulations necessary to channel private capital at scale and at speed. In short, the intention–action gap has widened and the risk that the climate crisis becomes unmanageable has risen. However, on the positive side, and as stated in part two, the zeitgeist has irrevocably changed. A significant majority of countries and industries now recognizes the need to take decisive action and make further commitments. Talk is easy but, now, the weather eye of activists, public opinion and, increasingly, regulators will make sure they keep them.

2.3.3. The conundrum of climate action

Except for a few diehard climate sceptics, nobody can disagree with Nicholas Stern's statement that "the costs of inaction on climate [are] far greater than the costs of action".[53] That said, there is no need to beat around the bush: climate action is hard, complex and often messy.

Why is there such a huge chasm between aspirations and policies? Why does climate action seem so intractable and why is it so difficult to put into place measures and policies that could effectively mitigate the risk of environmental degradation and climate change? There are essentially two (intertwined) reasons. One pertains to the difficulty of implementing the requisite measures, which often boils down to the nitty-gritty. The other has to do with climate justice and the perception that current measures are unfair by penalizing those who are the least responsible for the problem.

The transition to clean energy and the multiple innovations required to decarbonize our planet are two potentially gigantic opportunities in the medium and long term: they will underpin a "new growth strategy" (as Ursula von der Leyen said when presenting the European Green Deal) and create millions of jobs. But in the short term, they also carry a cost and associated political risks. Because (as referred to earlier) of the predominance of oil and gas in our global energy mix, transitioning to clean energy initially equates to what economists call a "negative supply shock" that will trigger energy price inflation (as already made evident in the fall of 2021). Moving forward, the absolute necessity to put a global price on carbon emissions will contribute further to energy inflation. Whatever the price put on carbon emissions (the IMF estimates an increase from $3 a tonne now to $75 in 2030,[54] much less than Nordhaus thinks is necessary), the cost of carbon will add a few percentage points to inflation – as just one example, from 0.6 to 2 in the United Kingdom, according to the Bank of England.[55] This will impact the fiscal positions in the countries that put into place programmes to protect the most vulnerable households from the effects of energy inflation, and will render the task of climate policy-making more arduous.

The episode of the "Yellow Vests" in France is a reminder of the ever-present risk of social unrest when tackling climate change. The introduction in 2018 of a small fuel-tax increase ignited the *Gilets Jaunes* crisis by hitting low- and middle-income workers disproportionately, as they have no choice but to commute to work by car. This illustrates a point emphasized in section 2.5: every major transition from one system to another creates winners and losers. The energy transition and the fight against climate change are no exception. Unless complex issues of redistribution, labour market implications and fairness are considered in the elaboration of climate policy, the buy-in from citizens "who worry more about the end of the month than the end of the world" (the leitmotiv of the *Gilets Jaunes* movement) won't happen, fuelling discontent and a societal backlash against climate action.

This time disconnect between short-term pain and long-term gains explains the prevalence of the "not in my term of office" (NIMTOF) syndrome among certain decision-makers. The NIMTOF acronym that was coined in the early days (2005) of the Global Risks Network at the World Economic Forum describes the position of some policy-makers and business leaders who do not pursue a given policy or strategy while they are at the helm, knowing it is necessary but preferring to pass the baton and the buck to their successor. It's a common human trait and a sign of our human frailty. Some decision-makers perceive the likelihood of a future possible disaster as being beyond the threshold of their immediate concerns and wind up thinking: "by the time the climate catastrophe bites us hard, I'll be gone so I'd better leave it to those who follow me". Leadership is about making tough and difficult decisions in uncertain circumstances, but action about climate change is such a momentous challenge with such complex ramifications that it may be "easier" for a political leader elected for five years or a business executive (whose time at the top rarely exceeds five years) to wait for the next leader to do the hard job.

The task of leaders and decision-makers is complicated further by three specific groups who question the pertinence of climate change policies or have a vested interest in preventing them from happening or disregarding them.

(1) The first group is composed by those who do not recognize or simply deny the science of climate change. According to numerous surveys conducted in various regions of the world, a significant number of people still believe that human-driven climate change is not occurring. The United States is at the epicentre of climate science denial: 30% of Americans doubt that human-caused climate change exists at all and 10% claim that the world's climate is not changing, a view mostly held by those on the political right who are more susceptible to disbelieve science and embrace conspiracy theo-

ries.[56] Such attitudes exist all over the world, but the number of doubters and deniers in other countries is smaller than in the US. Doubters and deniers are a substantial stumbling block nonetheless, because they feed polarization and slow (or even prevent) policy. Climate change is now one of the most politically polarized issues in many countries. This inevitably makes policy much more difficult.

(2) The second group is formed by people who recognize the importance of climate change policies but don't want them to directly impact their way of life. This is the climate equivalent of the "not in my backyard" (NIMBY) movement. Decarbonizing our economies requires replacing fossil fuels with renewables like wind, solar and other zero- or low-carbon energies that not everybody likes to see in their backyard. Daily, local newspapers report about resistance on the ground, including from some environmental groups, that prevents or slows such developments. Not knowing the merits of the case and without passing judgement, it can reasonably be argued that the vote in Maine in November 2021 against a 145-mile energy transmission project destined to bring clean Canadian hydropower to New England, because it would have disrupted the state's woodlands,[57] belongs to this category. Such issues illustrate the complex trade-offs that local and regional politicians face when having to choose between the transition to clean energy and the preservation of natural sites. On a broader level, a survey conducted in 10 countries just before COP26 epitomizes the problem with

personal attitudes when confronted with climate change and environmental degradation. It found that global citizens are concerned by the climate emergency, but a majority believe they are already doing more to preserve the planet than anyone else, including their government, and few are willing to make significant lifestyle changes. Three-fourths (76%) of those surveyed said they would accept stricter environmental rules and regulations, but almost half (46%) felt that there was no real need for them to change their personal habits.[58]

(3) The third group is a motley crowd of "human predators" who threaten, legally or not, the Indigenous communities whose lands contain a large portion of the world's remaining forests and some of the healthiest functioning ecosystems. Their territories are a fundamental component of the nature-based solution to sequester carbon and maintain effective ecosystems, but they are endangered by industrial farmers, miners, loggers and sometimes animal-parts traffickers and drug smugglers. This phenomenon is particularly evident in the last remaining major nature sanctuaries like the Amazon and the Congo Basin.

2.3.4. Climate justice

Environmental degradation and climate change harm disproportionately those least responsible for causing it, whether it's about countries (the rich world versus developing and emerging nations), generations (the young and future ones versus the old), or wealth and income (the wealthiest members of society versus the others).[59]

This fundamental problem of asymmetry calls for solutions that are fair and just. This section focuses exclusively on the historical responsibilities for climate change and the global solution to "climate justice" because it adds to the complexity, and sometimes seeming intractability, of climate action. Chandran Nair made this point unequivocally during our conversation with him when he said:

> The global minority [i.e. the Western world] has released the vast majority of emissions as it progressed over the last 200 years and continues to emit many times more than the global majority [i.e. the rest of the world]. The US, for example, has emitted far more CO2 than any other country: a quarter of all emissions since 1751 have occurred there. Despite China's huge rise in emissions over the past decade, emissions per person still sit at less than half those of the US. Meanwhile the one billion people living in Sub-Saharan Africa each emit one-twentieth of the average person in the US. By not clearly attributing responsibility of the climate crisis to the over-consumptive lifestyles in minority countries, political refuge is provided, and inaction is allowed, enabling the situation to worsen and impact the entire planet for the sake of pleasure for the minority.[60]

The data shows the necessity to acknowledge this legacy, through the cumulative carbon emissions per capita from 1850 to 2021. During this period, Canadians emitted the most (1,751 tonnes per capita), followed by the Americans (1,547), the New Zealanders (1,388), the Russians (1,181) and the British (1,100). By contrast, during that same period, the Chinese emitted 197 tonnes per capita and the Indians 61 tonnes.[61] Today, the Chinese and the Indians are among the largest world emitters in absolute terms, but the ranking in relative terms (that is, emissions per capita) is still dominated by the Americans.

To a substantial extent, this issue can explain why some emerging countries feel "entitled" to free-ride the efforts of some rich countries. Why should they expect, as so many policy-makers and analysts state, to forgo their development efforts to keep emissions low if they bear no or very little responsibility for the current climate crisis? Nair sees this effort to cut emissions globally as a form of "eco-imperialism", which he thinks is particularly obvious in the agenda to advance a net-zero 2050 world. In his opinion, "The collective push for carbon neutrality that the International Energy Agency has termed 'Net Zero Emissions by 2050 (NZE2050)' is fundamentally misleading and unachievable. It is simply not a viable global solution" because it "relies on a mixture of market-based mechanisms and technology quick-fixes (...) which have been developed for richer nations [but won't] work for the global majority [the non-Western world]" for reasons that are both technical and political. His argument is the following: "The main components of NZE2050 concern the conversion from fossil fuels to renewable energy, the use of carbon capture and sequestration, and carbon offsetting. (...) These methods may work in part for a country or a region (e.g. the EU) but they cannot be part of a global solution (...) [because they are not possible] in poor countries (global majority countries) within the 30-year timeframe needed to address the climate challenge. (...) These countries need requisite energy to build their nations and to provide basic needs for their large unserved populations. This cannot be circumvented or 'leapfrogged' by the technology-based methods inherent in NZE2050 – if global minority countries cannot implement CO2-reducing tech on a large scale, how could global majority countries achieve this?"[62]

For Nair, and many others who comment about climate policies, this divergence between the rich world and emerging countries will constitute a major, if not insurmountable, stumbling block in our collective quest for a solution, unless another more positive or "fairer" narrative replaces that of "us versus them". According to Nair, "The truth is that each nation and region will have different trajectories to take in the coming decades: the developed world will struggle to placate its populations when the need for reduced resource use and lowered emissions comes to bear, while the developing world will continue to struggle to provide security and meet the basic needs for its populations as the impacts of climate change worsen."

2.4. Geopolitics

The pandemic has exacerbated the geopolitical fault lines that were apparent before it struck. It seems that the 21st century is likely to be a period devoid of an absolute hegemon, during which no one power gains absolute dominance. In consequence, power and influence will be redistributed chaotically and, in some cases, grudgingly. In the next few decades, the world will be less secure and less stable than it was in the recent past. It will be marked by a sharp return to great power competition, exhibiting the features of a zero-sum game ("I win – you lose") and resembling a chessboard on which the rival must be defeated. The chaotic end of multilateralism, the current vacuum of global cooperation and the rise of various forms of nationalism and populist regimes will make it more difficult to find common ground when a crisis erupts. Today, when it could be argued the need is greater than ever, no new global order is in sight – just a chaotic transition to greater uncertainty and volatility.

This section focuses on the growing rivalry between the US and China. Many other important issues beset the world of geopolitics, like the rise of illiberalism, nationalism and populism; the weaponization of cyber or migration and other forms of hybrid warfare; the lack of effective international cooperation; and the increase in the number of fragile and failing states. However, the rising and seemingly intractable rivalry between China and the US represents the greatest geopolitical concern of our times, for two reasons: (1) the rivalry has the potential to generate global repercussions on an unprecedented scale and in a multiplicity of domains; and (2) no global issue can be significantly addressed without a modicum of cooperation between the two rivals. The rationale that underpins their current confrontation can be captured by the metaphor of the Thucydides Trap[63] – the structural tension that inevitably occurs when a rising power (China) challenges the ruling hegemon (the US). This confrontation will be a source of global messiness, disorder and uncertainty for years to come because, irrespective of whether one "likes" the US or not, the questioning of its global role and its progressive disengagement from the international scene are bound to increase international volatility. More and more, countries that tended to rely on global public goods provided by the US hegemon (for the fight against international terrorism, sea-lane security and other global issues) will now have to tend their own backyards themselves. As a result, the geopolitical landscape will suffer from a "global order deficit". The recent phenomenon of medium-sized powers becoming much more assertive and pursuing their own agenda is a concrete manifestation of this. The examples of Turkey's actions in the Caucasus, Belarus' on the border with the EU, Pakistan's in Afghanistan or Saudi Arabia's in Yemen come to mind. All, while regional in nature, are bad for global stability, as they make the world more dangerous and more confusing. Moving forward, unless individual nations and international organizations succeed in finding solutions to collaborate better at the global level, we risk entering an "age of entropy" in which retrenchment, resentment, fragmentation, anger and parochialism increasingly define our world, making it less intelligible and more disorderly.

For all these reasons, in the years to come, the quality of the relationship between China and the US will be the overpowering factor determining most of the global outcome, geopolitically of course, but in other areas as well. The multifaceted nature of their interdependence touches upon all the most important aspects of international affairs: climate change and the environment, global economic growth and financial stability, international trade and investment, conflicts and regional instability, the future of tech governance, the deep-seated conflict between authoritarianism and liberal democracies, the race for space dominance – and this list is not exhaustive. The outcome of each of these major issues depends heavily on the capacity of China and the US to cooperate. But after 40 years of strategic engagement, the two countries appear to have reached the conclusion that they cannot bridge the ideological, political and strategic divides that separate them. Far from uniting the two giants, the pandemic did the exact opposite by exacerbating their rivalry and intensifying competition between them. As a result, they are now diverging, even though their deep economic and financial interdependence suggests that a full decoupling would prove to be an exceedingly difficult and painful proposition. A complete separation would indeed entail considerable costs on both sides, as illustrated by two examples: US trade with China represents more than $500 billion while China holds more than $1 trillion of US Treasury securities (around 4% of total US sovereign debt). The same logic applies to most US traditional allies for whom China has now become the main trading partner. For the EU, Japan, South Korea, Saudi Arabia and the UAE, being asked to "take sides" between China or the US is an almost impossible proposition. "We can't afford to do it," confided to us a Middle Eastern policy-maker. Most business leaders of global companies would concur. For years to come, they will have to straddle the divide as best they can. This risks being an uncomfortable position.

For realists and other proponents of great-power politics, this rising rivalry should come as no surprise. "Who can blame Chinese leaders for seeking to dominate Asia and become the most powerful state on the planet?" asks political scientist John Mearsheimer. He adds:

> Certainly not the United States, which pursued a similar agenda, rising to become a hegemon in its own region and eventually the most secure and influential country in the world. And today, the United States is also acting just as realist logic would predict. Long opposed to the emergence of other regional hegemons, it sees China's ambitions as a direct threat and is determined to check the country's continued rise. The inescapable outcome is competition and conflict. Such is the tragedy of great-power politics (...) Most Americans do not recognize that Beijing and Washington are following the same playbook, because they believe the United States is a noble democracy that acts differently from authoritarian and ruthless countries such as China. But that

> is not how international politics works. All great powers, be they democracies or not, have little choice but to compete for power in what is at root a zero-sum game. This imperative motivated both superpowers during the Cold War. It motivates China today and would motivate its leaders even if it were a democracy. And it motivates American leaders, too, making them determined to contain China.[64]

Not everybody will concur with this logic of the "realist" school of international affairs that a conflict is inevitable. Undoubtedly, the competition between the two superpowers will be ever more intense, but is an actual armed conflict likely? Great powers seldom express a willingness to go to war, but history provides many examples of how they can stumble into it. Previous occurrences of the Thucydides Trap show that, when a dominant power starts worrying and feeling insecure, it may also start overreacting and miscalculate. Similarly, the emerging power might feel emboldened by the prospect of dominance, become overconfident and do the same: overreact and miscalculate. In one of our conversations, Niall Ferguson observed that, "It is all too easy to see a sequence of events unfolding that could lead to another unnecessary war, most probably over Taiwan, which Mr Xi covets and which America is (ambiguously) committed to defend against invasion – a commitment that increasingly lacks credibility as the balance of military power shifts in East Asia." For his part, Xue Lan put the responsibility of the two countries falling into the Thucydides Trap squarely on the shoulders of the US: "Scholars already warned us quite some time ago about this potential trap. But still, what is happening between the US and China shows that, despite the warning, US domestic politics works in a way that really makes it impossible for any politician to escape from such a trap. People had hoped that a new US administration might change things but, unfortunately, they were wrong. The new administration is more or less following a similar path. It's not as simple as something that any individual politician can get us out of."

Most narratives about the current and future relationship between China and the US tend to be "bearish". Why so? Because in the foreseeable future, the two countries are likely to evolve in a way that will make them less prone to seek ways to collaborate effectively with each other.

The reasons are the following: at this juncture in history, neither the US nor China has an incentive to tone the confrontation down.

The US, after decades of unrivalled global dominance, is currently engaged in a process of "strategic contraction".[65] It may continue to dominate the geopolitical landscape for many more years, but its absolute supremacy is now gone, forcing its leadership to manage an inevitable, gradual decline as gently as it can. That said, as Ferguson put it, "the retreat from global dominance is rarely a peaceful process" – an observation that the

American pull-out from Afghanistan made painfully vivid. As the global hegemon renounces global policing, it incites all sorts of declared enemies and other protagonists to test its resolve and emboldens them to make trouble elsewhere. In addition, doubts have been expressed by many American and foreign observers about the way in which the US system is evolving and whether its social fabric and political structures are as resilient now as they were in the past. They worry about whether the US society and its system of government have been structurally impaired by polarization and cronyism. Moisés Naím echoed such concerns when saying:

> The next mid-term elections in the United States will be an important test of that. We'll see many illiberal initiatives and ideas put into play and gaining support. I predict that funding of the US military will be more contested. The country spends about $738 billion each year in defence, which is more than the next 10 countries combined. And there was a peaceful coexistence with the notion that the Pentagon can spend limitless money with no constraints. But what did that buy the United States or the world over the last 20 years in Afghanistan or in Iraq? When was the last time the United States was victorious in a large-scale operation? Is that worth spending $738 billion a year? That debate will be very important. In the past, the lobbyists and the mili-

> tary–industrial–financial complex took care of protecting that budget because they ate and profited from that budget. That may become more difficult in the future. High military spending will not go away but it will be more contested and politically costly.

As for China, its leader(ship) exudes confidence about the country's political system, its position vis-à-vis the US and the long-term stability of the Chinese Communist Party. It seems determined to reclaim what it sees as its rightful global position at a time when it has the economic and military capabilities to be more assertive. After decades of uninterrupted rapid economic and military development, the country has now reached an inflection point: growth is slowing, and challenges are mounting in a global environment perceived by some to be more hostile to Chinese interests.[66] It is for this reason that if the country "is to become a 'modern socialist nation' by 2035, Xi believes bold action must be taken now".[67] But many analysts point out that there is nothing inexorable about China's rise to global dominance. Its population is ageing very fast and its workforce shrinking, while over-indebtedness and the deflating of the property bubble could trigger a major and abrupt contraction in growth. If so, some experts argue that it is its weaknesses rather than its strengths that would pose the greatest dangers to geopolitical stability. Their argument is that if the economic difficulties grow, China's leadership might choose to stoke nationalism by escalating confrontations with the US, with Taiwan as the most tempting target.

In short, there is as little chance of Chinese leaders abandoning their value system to become more like the Americans would like them to be as there is of American leaders abandoning theirs to become more like the Chinese would like them to be. In the coming years, a peaceful coexistence between the two rivals and the demonstrable ability to collaborate on some global issues like climate change would be the best possible outcome, but it is not a given. As the hedge fund manager Ray Dalio commented, "There are five kinds of war, and they are not all shooting wars. There's a trade war, a technology war, a geopolitical war, a capital war, and there could be a military war. We are certainly in varying degrees in the first four of those, and there's good reason to worry about the fifth type."[68]

2.5. Society

Among the many societal challenges we collectively face, the most damaging and deep-rooted is inequality. As UN Secretary-General António Guterres puts it, "Inequality defines our time."[69] Its manifestations are so multifaceted and have reached such proportions to address that it demands nothing short of a redefinition of our social contract.

COVID-19 has exacerbated pre-existing conditions of inequality, making them worse in several respects. The first was to magnify the challenge of social inequalities by spotlighting the shocking disparities in the degree of risk to which different social classes are exposed (the upper and middle classes have been much less affected by COVID than members of the working class). The second was to expose the profound disconnect between the essential nature and innate value of a job done and the economic recompense it commands. Put another way: COVID made it plain that we value least economically the individuals that society needs the most in times of crisis (like nurses, delivery personnel or cleaners). The third was to observe that the ultra-accommodative monetary policies pursued around the world increased wealth inequalities by fuelling asset prices, most notably in financial markets and property. According to Credit Suisse's *Global wealth report 2021*, wealth differences between adults widened in 2020 in most countries and for the world as a whole. The global number of millionaires expanded by 5.2 million to reach 56.1 million. As a result, an adult now needs more than $1 million to belong to the global top 1%. The ultra-high-net-worth group added 24% more members, the highest rate of increase since 2003.[70] These observations strike a "social" chord in our imagination. One of the (many) reasons why "Squid Games" became such a planetary success is that the series tapped a sense familiar to people all over the world. It seems that prosperity in rich countries has become increasingly difficult to achieve and that excessive indebtedness to keep up with the Joneses condemns many to a life of misery. More generally, a deep sense of unfairness is engulfing much of the world. More and more, the truth is percolating that it's much harder than in the recent past to climb the social ladder for those who are born poor and with little social capital. The system seems biased in an ingrained manner against the less privileged members of society. In our conversation, the political philosopher Martin O'Neill summed this up as follows:

> The societies we live in – the kind of economies, the institutional structures within which we live together – have gone badly wrong in the degree of inequality they've allowed to develop (...). In societies like my own (the United Kingdom) and other developed countries, the degree of inequality is now so severe that it really threatens the legitimacy of our societies' institutional structures. But the kind of inequality we should worry about is not just about inequality regarding income or wealth distribution – it's not captured just by the Gini coefficient within a society – but the problem is that we've got multidimensional inequality within many of these societies that is inconsistent with all the citizens of a society having the full set of entitlements that equal citizens ought to have. That sounds a bit abstract, but I suppose one way of thinking about inequality, and the things that might trouble us about it, aren't just facts about economic distribution, but also facts about the distribution of power, voice, status, influence and opportunities; it's the combination of all those dimensions of inequality together that should trouble us.

Measuring global inequality is difficult. Branko Milanovic, one of the world's leading authorities in the domain states that:

> Global inequality has been on a downward trend since about the mid- or late-1990s. (…) This is thanks to high rates of growth in Asian countries that were relatively poor, particularly China and, more recently, India. These two giants – I call them "Sumo wrestlers" of global inequality – are wrestling global inequality down. So, it is not true that today global inequality is the highest it's ever been; it's significantly lower than it was in the 1960s through the 1980s. Some people either don't know that or argue that if we take absolute income gaps, then, yes, the distances have increased because the GDP of the world has gone up very significantly and the absolute income gaps between individuals have increased as well. In that sense, yes, I agree [that the world was never as unequal as it is today], but one should realize that these absolute distances always go up when the GDP of a country or, in this case, the world, goes up. Absolute income gaps are much greater in today's United States than they were during slavery. But "absolute" is, as this example shows, a wrong metric to study inequality over time.

The fact that inequalities between countries may have been decreasing is of little comfort to people who feel victims of unfairness in terms of inequalities, because, in the end, it is inequality within countries that matters to citizens. In that respect, the evidence of a rise in inequality is incontrovertible. The most recent *World Inequality Report*[71] shows that almost everywhere in the world (Europe is the exception), the share of the bottom 50% in total earnings is less than 15% (and less than 10% in Latin America, Sub-Saharan Africa and the MENA region – the Middle East and North Africa) while the share of the richest 10% is over 40% and, in many of the regions, closer to 60%. In terms of wealth, the share of the bottom 50% of the world in total global wealth is 2%, while the share of the top 10% is 76%. What is striking is the extreme concentration of the economic power in the hands of a very small minority of super-rich. The wealth of the top 10% globally, which constitutes the middle class in rich countries and the merely rich in poor countries, is in fact growing slower than the world average, but the top 1% is growing much faster; between 1995 and 2021, they captured 38% of the global increment in wealth, while the bottom 50% captured a mere 2%. Over the same period, the share of wealth owned by the global top 0.1% rose from 7% to 11%. More generally, the data shows that inequalities of wealth, of income, of opportunity, of gender, of race, of education and of generation have all been exacerbated during the pandemic.[72] Hence, the legacy of the COVID-19 pandemic will be a more unequal world.[73]

Furthermore, inequality and the unfairness that underpins it are clear for all to see. By contrast to a decade or so ago, we now live in a transparent era, moving fast into a world of incessant and almost universal observation. Technology is making our every gesture easy to track, and we must therefore come to terms with the notion that privacy no longer exists: our personal and professional data are progressively becoming fully monitored, visible to many, and as such transparent. By providing access to relevant information and sometimes simply revealing the truth, transparency (fostered by whistle blowers) makes the public and, in particular, the young generation more sensitive to the issue of inequality and more aware of "misbehaving" on the part of some public leaders, corporate titans and wealthy individuals. Nothing made this more explicit than the nearly 12 million confidential financial records contained in the Pandora Papers leaked in 2021 (preceded in 2016 by the Panama Papers and in 2017 by the Paradise Papers). They throw light on the system of "legal corruption" that occurs on a vast scale at the highest levels of politics and business. Most depressingly, they reveal that the policy-makers empowered to bring the system to an end can also be among those with a vested interest in prolonging it. More than 330 of the people exposed in the Pandora Papers are politicians from 90 countries, including 35 current and former heads of state or government, some of whom were elected after flamboyant anti-corruption campaigns. In the opinion of an academic certified as a wealth manager so that he could research that industry from inside, tax havens are not set up to avoid taxes but to help some members of the elite to avoid the rule of law imposed on the rest of the population. Thus, the offshore financial industry generates much of the economic and political inequality destabilizing the world.[74] As the public becomes aware of these leaks, the foundational premise of equity – i.e. that governments serve the people and apply the rule of law equally – is seriously undermined and ultimately destroyed. As a result, people become angry, convinced that the system is rigged, and lose faith or hope that things might one day get better for them. A toxic sentiment of unfairness permeates their lives.

In light of this, it should come as no surprise that the rise is inequality is accompanied by a concomitant increase in dissatisfaction, often expressed via demonstrations and social unrest. The global increase in protests began years before the pandemic, particularly after the financial crisis of 2008 when demonstrations coalesced around the theme of the growing disparity between the haves and the have-nots. At that time, policies centred on fiscal austerity galvanized popular anger. More than 10 years later, the pandemic has triggered an upsurge in social unrest and protests around the world. According to the Armed Conflict Location & Event Data Project, between 2019 and 2020, the number of demonstrations globally increased by 7% despite lockdowns and other governmental measures put into place to limit public gatherings.[75] Evidently, the policy responses to the pandemic played an important role in fuelling this dissatisfaction: many demonstrations were organized against the lockdowns and vaccination policies, but there is more than that. As told by a young Colombian activist: "It's people showing the discontent that they have been feeling for a long time."[76] The COVID demonstrations, like those that preceded it, also boil down to a deeper sense of disillusionment: it seems that the social contract that binds people together and shapes their relations with their governments is failing. In the words of a political scientist, "The governments of today are incapable of offering both representative *and* effective governance. (…) While many demonstrations explicitly invoke the pandemic, the bigger, latent concern is the inability of modern governments to serve the majority of their populations, especially the middle and poorer classes."[77]

Rising concerns about inequality and the profound sentiment of dissatisfaction, if not anger, that it provokes will prompt many societies around the world to redefine the terms of their social contract. Broadly defined, the "social contract" refers to the (often implicit) set of arrangements and expectations that govern the relations between individuals and institutions. Put simply, it is the "glue" that binds us, our societies, together; without it, the social fabric unravels. The growing general recognition is that the social contract in many countries around the world is broken, and that its multiple elements "from cradle to grave"[78] need to change.

For decades, pretty much everywhere, the social contract has slowly and almost imperceptibly evolved in a direction that has forced individuals to assume greater responsibility for their individual lives and economic outcomes, leading large swathes of the population (most evidently in the low-income brackets) to conclude that the social contract was at best being eroded, if not in some cases breaking down entirely. Today, the fundamental reasons underpinning the loss of faith in our social contracts coalesce around issues of inequality, the ineffectiveness of most redistribution policies, a sense of exclusion and marginalization, and a general sentiment of unfairness. It is for this reason that many citizens have begun to denounce a breakdown of the social contract, expressing more and more forcefully a general loss of trust in institutions and leaders.[79] In some countries, this widespread exasperation has taken the form of both peaceful and violent demonstrations; in others, it has led to electoral victories for populist and extremist parties. Whichever form it takes, in almost all cases, the establishment's response has been left wanting – ill-prepared for the rebellion and out of ideas and policy levers to address the problem. Although they are complex, the policy solutions do exist (as we will see in chapter 3) and broadly consist in adapting the welfare state to today's world by empowering people and by responding to the demands for a fairer social contract. Over the past few years, several international organizations and think tanks have adjusted to this new reality and outlined proposals on how to make it happen.[80] The pandemic has marked a turning point by accelerating this transition. It has magnified and crystallized the issue and made a return to the pre-pandemic status quo impossible.

Which particular form might the new social contract take? There are no off-the-shelf, ready-to-use models because each potential solution depends upon the history and culture of the country to which it applies. For obvious reasons, a "good" social contract for China will be different from one for the US, which in turn will not resemble one for Denmark or Nigeria. However, they could all share some common features and principles, the absolute necessity for which has been made ever-more obvious by the social and economic consequences of the pandemic crisis. Two stand out: (1) a broader, if not universal, provision of social assistance, social insurance, healthcare and basic quality services; and (2) a move towards enhanced protection for workers in the form of mandatory benefits, a minimum decent wage and help to adapt to (the disruptive effects of) innovation. In addition, a critical aspect of a new social contract pertains to liberties and freedom, at least in democratic countries. There is a growing concern that the fight against this pandemic and the future ones will lead to the creation of permanent surveillance societies, an issue explored in more detail in the next section.

Collectively redefining the terms of our social contracts is an epochal task that binds the substantial challenges of the present moment to the hopes of the future. As Henry Kissinger reminded us, "The historic challenge for leaders is to manage the crisis while building the future. Failure could set the world on fire."[81] While reflecting on the contours we think a future social contract might follow, we ignore at our peril the opinion of the younger generation who will be asked to live with it. Their adherence is decisive and thus to better understand what they want, we must not forget to listen. This is all the more significant because the younger generation is likely to be more radical in its demands in the refashioning of our social contract. The pandemic has upended their lives, and a whole generation across the globe will be defined by economic insecurity and climate anxiety. They will bear these scars forever. Already the millennials (at least in the Western world) are worse off than their parents in terms of earnings, assets and wealth. They are less likely to own a home or have children than their parents were. Now, another generation (Gen Z) is entering a system that it sees as failing and that will be beset by long-standing problems revealed and exacerbated by the pandemic. As a college junior put it: "Young people have a deep desire for radical change because we see the broken path ahead."[82]

How will this generation respond? By proposing radical solutions, and often radical action, to prevent issues like social inequalities from worsening or the next disaster like climate change from striking (the young generations see both as two facets of the same coin: intergenerational inequality). It will most likely demand a radical alternative to the present course because its members are frustrated and dogged by a nagging belief that the current system has failed them and is fractured beyond repair. As a result, youth activism is increasing worldwide,[83] being revolutionized by social media that fosters mobilization to an extent that would have been impossible before.[84] It takes many different forms, ranging from non-institutionalized political participation to demonstrations and protests, and addresses inequalities in a multifaceted manner, seeing issues as diverse as income inequalities, climate change, economic reforms, gender equality and LGBTQ rights as part of a more general inequality problem. The young generation is firmly at the vanguard of social change. There is little doubt that it will be the catalyst for change.

2.6. Technology

Technology's contribution to our endeavours, both at the societal and individual levels, is always perceived as ambivalent. Some see it as the ultimate solution to the problems of humankind and a constant source of progress. Others are suspicious and defiant, concerned about the way in which technology can be used for nefarious purposes. Section 3.7 focuses on the former, with a particular emphasis on how the remarkable acceleration of technological innovation could help us move towards a future that is both environmentally and socially sustainable. This section will address the concerns of the latter. In the years to come, the issues, challenges and unknowns are indeed considerable about how we will collectively manage advances in technology (through regulation and other means) for the common good.

Changes in technology are not debatable: contrary to changes in complex adaptive systems like our societies, the economy or geopolitics that are always subject to interpretation, tech is different. Its changes are palpable and unfold before our very eyes. The landing on the moon, the internet, progress in medical science, ubiquitous mobile phones, drones, mRNA vaccines: these now exist for all to see. They are a reality and not reliant on value judgements. This may be the reason why many think tomorrow's world will be fundamentally the same as yesterday's just with the appendage of technological change. The historian Niall Ferguson is one such proponent who, when discussing future change, affirms that, "The underlying nature of human relationships – of love, friendship, power and enmity – will remain the same, [which is why] we can understand Thucydides and Shakespeare, because those fundamental human relationships don't actually change over time. What changes is technology."[85]

Some changes in technology make us techno-optimists, while others incline us to techno-pessimism. Sometimes the same technological change can be regarded optimistically by some and pessimistically by others. To a considerable extent, it is narratives that shape our perceptions of the opportunities and risks embedded in technological progress. Scientists tend to be careful when expressing a view about the future, but authors of science fiction are not. In this way, their trade helps us make imaginative leaps to plausible futures. Stories range from being disturbingly dystopian, like in Margaret Atwood's *The Handmaid's Tale*, to depicting exhilarating possibilities and a rather hopeful future, like in Liu Cixin's *The Three-Body Problem*. We unconsciously rely on them to make up our minds about tech. Potent narratives in literature, movies or comics (like the Japanese manga) have the power to instil fear or alternatively engender reassurance with regard to technology and innovation. Let's take as an example the new concept of metaverse – the immersive, virtual reality world that offers us the possibility to live our lives vicariously, as in a parallel digital universe populated by avatars. The word "metaverse", now embraced by big tech companies like Facebook and Microsoft, was coined in a novel written by Neal Stephenson (*Snow Crash*, published in 1992). The book's tone was rather dystopian (the novel takes place in an anarcho-capitalist universe ravaged by hyperinflation) and depicts a virtual space shared by both humans and digital "daemons". Thirty years later, the term "metaverse" has become shorthand for a series of interconnected virtual worlds whose sophistication should rapidly grow. The metaverse will contain environments where we will earn money, forge relationships and have all sorts of different experiences that could enrich our lives or quite the opposite. Opinions diverge, but all those who think about the metaverse agree that it will have a profound impact on how our societies function, our economies run and our political systems operate. The distinction between being offline and online will become increasingly blurred and harder to identify, and the meaning of reality itself will evolve (it might become extended – XR – combining augmented, virtual and mixed realities). There is no doubt that this whole process will be a transformative one. Some loathe the idea. Others embrace it with enthusiasm.

The same applies to AI. It inspires both fear and hope – sentiments often forged by our own cultural biases. Research on AI narratives shows that a subset of Western narratives has been disproportionately influential in the dystopian visions of AI across the English-speaking world.[86] "We get ideas about what AI should look like from Hollywood, that's where the idea of the humanoid robot comes from (…). We did a survey in the UK. If people are concerned about AI, they cite 'The Terminator'." By contrast, Japanese attitudes to AI are dramatically less dystopian because of the unique cultural history of robots in

Japanese manga. Two of the country's most famous animated series, "Astro Boy" and "Doraemon", have been around since the 1960s and have deeply influenced people's positive associations with AI. Astro Boy is a little android with superhuman powers who coexists happily with humans, while Doraemon is a cute blue cat who happens to be a robot and who travels back in time to save a young boy. "Compared with 'The Terminator', this is such a different perspective on what AI could be (…). Having that different narrative history completely changes the way in which people think about tech."[87]

Beyond the implicit biases, our appreciation of the risks and opportunities associated with technology are distorted by the sheer velocity of its progress. As stated in section 2.1, the speed of change never ceases to take us by surprise. Isaac Asimov's aphorism that "science gathers knowledge faster than society gathers wisdom"[88] is more than 30 years old, but it's probably truer now than it's ever been. Science, innovation and technology are moving incredibly fast in an expanding multiplicity of fields that interact with each other in complex and often disconcerting ways. So much is happening in each sub-discipline that scientists confess it's very challenging to keep an eye on how the broad tech landscape is evolving. What appears hard for scientists is virtually impossible to grasp for most laymen. The news is awash with terms like "gene synthesis revolution", "cyberwarfare", "fusion and fission technologies", "additive manufacturing", "internet of things (IoT)", "quantum computing" or "neurotechnology", but how many of us can comprehend the details and significance of what these mean and entail? How are public policies supposed to adjust to these remarkable new developments that harness so much potential but portend such great danger if they fall in the wrong hands? How capable are legislators and regulators to enact the right laws and rules? And can they work together at the global level?

A few decades ago, the cognitive psychologist and economist Herbert Simon neatly summed up the problem of ambivalence when observing that, "There are no morals about technology at all. Technology expands our ways of thinking about things, expands our ways of doing things. If we are bad people, we use technology for bad purposes, and if we are good people, we use it for good purposes."[89] The simple truth is that any technology can be used for good or for ill, and that no technology comes up with its own purposely designed value system. Humans decide.

This section focuses on what the major or key concerns and worries ought to be. They abound, ranging from the effect that generative neural networks could have on political polarization, to the risk that quantum computing might unscramble a slew of data already encrypted by business, or risks that are more societal in nature, like "surveillance capitalism".[90] The (arbitrary) focus here is on just three major potential risks, acute and possibly immensely consequential, that stem from technological innovation. All three relate to broad technological categories whose commonality is that they are or could soon be weaponized. In each, the risks can be amplified by those emanating from the other two (AI, for example, can make cyber-risks much more acute by enabling vulnerabilities to be found). The first, associated with digitalization, is clearly identifiable: cybercrime. The second, about the contribution of AI to warfare, is emerging. The third, linked to synthetic biology, is still nascent. The bottom line: for all their immensely positive potential, the interlocking technologies of digitalization, AI and synthetic biology present equally significant risks.[91]

2.6.1. Cyber-risks

The risks associated with cybercrime are the most current and tangible because they have affected or will affect most of us and millions of companies around the world. Cybercrime, cyberattacks and ransomware are on the increase globally, becoming ever more targeted and "strategic" in nature. Estimating the true cost of global cybercrime is impossible due to its diffuse and hidden nature, but some industry sources put it at $6 trillion in 2021, rising to $10.5 trillion annually by 2025.[92] Cyberattacks, launched by faceless hackers hidden behind their computers (or sometimes in certain states in military facilities), have very real consequences and can cause very real harm. To provide just one specific example that is almost five years old, North Korean hackers in 2017 exploited a vulnerability in the Microsoft Windows operating system that infected over 300,000 computer systems in 150 countries with a malicious virus called WannaCry. It affected individuals, companies and state agencies, including the British National Health Service, which had to cancel almost

20,000 appointments, causing around $100 million in damages. Experts estimated that the total cost of the global disruption reached about $4 billion.[93] Ransomware attacks, almost unknown a few years ago, are now pervasive. Worldwide, they will probably amount to more than 700 million by the end of this year, an increase of about 130% compared to last year.[94] They can inflict tremendous damage on a company but also exercise a much broader negative economic impact, like the attack in June 2021 on the meatpacking company JBS that cut off 20% of US beef- and pork-packing capacity, leading to a temporary shortage and higher prices. Analysts concur cybercrime is a game of whack-a-mole that will intensify because these invisible attacks make retaliation very difficult. For years, policy-makers have warned about the possibility of a "cyber–Pearl Harbor" that would inflict devastating damage on a country or an industry's critical digital infrastructure. We are there. Sophisticated "private" cyber actors are now capable of disabling most companies or large entities like a city or a network. As for state-supported cyber actors, they can do the same for an entire country.

It is exceedingly difficult to extend and apply norms and rules that can ensure safety in the digital world. To a large extent, international laws govern the conduct of war and nuclear weapons, but this is not yet the case for the cyberspace. The current unwillingness to cooperate at the international level compounded by the effect of asymmetry (it's not always easy to identify the perpetrator of a cyberattack) make it hard to envisage any real progress in the foreseeable future.

2.6.2. AI and warfare

Cybercrime and cyberattacks take place in the digital realm, without shots being fired or bombs being launched. This is fundamentally different from modern warfare, which is fast becoming cyber – combining deadly force with digital capabilities. In March 2021, the UN reported that for the first time ever, military-grade autonomous drones that can fly themselves to a specific location, pick their own targets and kill without the assistance of a remote human operator had been deployed on the battlefield in Libya in March 2020. Such drones can be operated both autonomously and manually, and use "machine learning" and "real-time image processing" against their targets.[95] At the end of September 2020, the conflict in Nagorno-Karabakh displayed the first evidence of an interstate modern warfare being partially cyber. Autonomous killer drones capable of deadly force were used on the Azeri side and secured victory against the Armenians. There is no doubt that such weapons (which already exist alongside biomimetic weapons) will become increasingly prevalent in modern conflicts, posing numerous ethical concerns and dilemmas in terms of international humanitarian law that governs armed conflict and for which there are currently no responses.

Stuart Russell, a British pioneering AI researcher who's spent the past 10 years trying to ban AI from being used to locate and kill human targets, warns that AI weapons are developing fast and in a completely unregulated manner. "You can buy them today. They are advertised on the web. (...) A lethal AI-powered quadcopter could be as small as a tin of shoe polish ... about three grammes of explosive are enough to kill a person at close range. A regular container could hold a million lethal weapons, and they can all be sent to do their work at once, so the inevitable endpoint is that autonomous weapons become cheap, selective, weapons of mass destruction."[96] Therefore, in his informed opinion, like that of many other prominent scientists and ethicists in the field of AI, the proliferation of AI weapons poses an imminent and existential threat. To counter it, Max Tegmark, a MIT professor who co-founded the Future of Life Institute, a think tank that works on reducing global catastrophic and existential risk from powerful technologies,[97] has suggested implementing an international moratorium on autonomous lethal weapons. Scientists in other countries are pursuing a similar route, like the 400 German AI researchers who published an open letter to the German Government asking that its armed forces stop developing such systems and recommending that, "such dehumanization of life and death decision-making by autonomous weapons systems must be outlawed worldwide".[98]

But worldwide, governments capable of developing such AI weapons are against a ban (which, for obvious reasons, are only voiced in countries that allow freedom of speech). Nations should develop consultations and arms-control agreements, but it's hard to understand what arms control for AI might look like. "Unlike nuclear and conventional weapons – which are large, visible, clunky, and countable – swarms of AI-enabled drones or torpedoes are harder to verify, and the algorithms that guide them are even more elusive."[99] Unless a sense of self-preservation prompts national authorities to act in concert and agree on a set of common standards, like making a specified minimum weight and explosive size compulsory so that autonomous weapons can't be wielded as swarms from the back of a van, the risk of AI lethal weapons becoming as ubiquitous as guns is very real.

2.6.3. Synthetic biology

It is often said that the 19th century was the century of chemistry, the 20th century of physics and the 21st century will be that of biology – a century during which we will re-engineer biological systems to meet human demands. We are at the dawn of the genetics revolution, having sequenced the human genome, turned adult cells into stem cells, understood how to rewrite the genetic code of any living cell, and reduced the cost of hacking genes by a factor of millions. Besides, we already have a successful example proving that synthetic biology delivers on its promises. Just as World War II accelerated electronics, the pandemic has propelled the genetics revolution towards new frontiers. When COVID-19 struck, it triggered an immediate and furious search for a vaccine. Those that came first are mRNA vaccines that insert synthetic strings of genetic code that are computer-modelled into our bodies. Instead of triggering our immune system with a traditional vaccine that injects a weakened, dead or partial pathogen, mRNA vaccines instruct our cells to produce the spike protein of the SARS-CoV-2 virus. By doing so, they "transform our bodies into personalized manufacturing plants producing an otherwise foreign object to trigger our natural immune response. This approach will soon create a whole new platform for fighting cancers and other diseases, as well as for providing enhancements ever more profound than vaccination."[100]

The potential of such Promethean technologies seems amazing and infinite. Transforming our healthcare so that personalized treatments and predictive health issue modelling become possible; brewing animal proteins from cell cultures and generating energy from algae to save the planet: these and many other applications seem within reach. But so, too, does the possibility to use them for the wrong purpose – inadvertently, implicitly or with intent. The potential of synthetic biology is such that it's not hard to imagine what could go wrong. What if, in the case of a pandemic, we only inoculate citizens in the rich countries (not a far-fetched scenario)? What if we improve or prolong the life of only those who can afford it? What if we start discriminating against people based on their genetic information? What if soon anyone can make a virus from scratch? What if genetic manipulation of pre-implanted embryos leads to eugenics? What if a country or a malicious group decides to produce a dangerous, unknown synthetic pathogen? What if the next pandemic is lab-made? What if a pathogen is enhanced to increase transmissibility or its ability to cause disease is augmented? These are a few common-sense questions for which we don't (yet) have an answer. The fundamental issue of how our newfound ability to manipulate life will impact our humanness challenges our beliefs, morals, religions and politics at their very core, and we are ill-prepared for that. As the naturalist E.O. Wilson said: "We have Palaeolithic emotions, medieval institutions and godlike technologies."[101] Indeed. The policy community is far behind in trying to keep up with the potential hurdles that might require regulation. John Steele, Nautilus' editor-in-chief, observed that:

> It's a very scary thing. Especially when the technology is becoming so easy to use. The gene-editing technology CRISPR is becoming easy to use. There are all sorts of genetic engineering threats out there that aren't regulated because the political and regulatory community can't keep up with them. It's a real threat. It's one of those great unknowns about, when we go into one of these technologies, what potential, unintended consequences come out the other side. (…) I think it's a huge concern. Everyone worries about where a certain technology can lead. It's on everybody's mind. And the speed of development makes the potential threats even more concerning, just because of the speed and sheer degree of invention that's going on every day.[102]

It is not a hyperbolic proposition to state that synthetic biology, like AI, is a sweeping force that will reshape our future by modifying how our cultures, societies and economies operate – and probably sooner than we realize. We are at the dawn of the genetics revolution, and when our DNA (that is, our code of life) becomes as readable, writable, usable and hackable as information technology, we'll be on the cusp of something much bigger than us. It is therefore essential to realize that "the choices we make today will be the difference between realizing breathtaking advances in human well-being and descending into a dangerous and potentially deadly genetic arms race".[103] If we fail to take significant regulatory action and do not collaborate at the international level, it will be both.

3. The Way Forward – Solutions

As already made clear, the global risks emanating from our five macro categories are not only consequential but also on the rise. In the years ahead, more shocks will disrupt our lives, threaten our societies, endanger our economies and imperil peace. The challenges we collectively face may seem overwhelming, yet there are reasons to remain hopeful about the future. "Only crises compel us to act," observed Sadhguru, and the pressing necessity to build a world that is more resilient, collaborative, sustainable and equitable is prompting us to do so. We find ourselves in the midst of rapid reinvention, rewriting as we go many of the rules that govern our economies and societies. In the words of Mariana Mazzucato, "We are on the cusp of a long-overdue paradigm shift." This chapter of the book captures these coming changes and some of the hopeful narratives built around them. They point to a way forward by bridging the gap between the world of ideas and that of practice and policy.

3.1. Collaboration and cooperation

Collaboration (working together to achieve a common goal) and cooperation (the action of achieving one's own goal as part of a common goal) are a broad domain of practice to which many academic disciplines as different as political science, anthropology, psychology, economics law, or biology have devoted countless books and articles. Our purpose is not to delve into the details of such a wide subject, but to explore a few narratives on what might expand our ability to collaborate and cooperate (with both terms henceforth used interdependently) and what this entails. The case is clear: global governance is faltering because of our rising inability to work together at the global and international levels. Yet, as expanded in part one, all the mounting problems we face are global in nature. Pandemics, climate change, biodiversity, geopolitics, trade and investment, economic growth, cybersecurity, tech governance – all these and other global issues can only be successfully addressed if done so in a collaborative fashion. Essentially, we should treat them as public goods. A peaceful world, a healthy world, a breathable world, a clean world, a fair world: each should be regarded as a global public good whose provision depends on our ability to cooperate globally. Such a pressing necessity was made obvious with COVID-19: no global state exists to deliver a vaccine to the entire world, so the effort to vaccinate as many people as possible falls upon international organizations whose power is constrained by competing national interests and a patchwork of fragmented agreements and initiatives negotiated between 200 sovereign states. It doesn't work. On 21 November 2021, the lack of global cooperation and the incessant bickering about burden sharing meant that only 54.7% of the world population was vaccinated. At the time of writing, the emergence and identification of the Omicron variant might prove to be a stark consequence of this failing.

Polarization, geopolitical rivalries, ethnic divides and social fractures make cooperation increasingly difficult. This said, as our global problems worsen, could it be that we realize there is no choice but to cooperate? Might we eventually come to the conclusion that unless we collaborate better, we are doomed? Might we finally understand that we all share one planet and that all our destinies are inextricably linked, that we are just a single civilization in a single biosphere? If so, might this realization unleash a burst of cooperation and creativity? Maybe, but the devil is in the details. As Martin Wolf ponders: "how might this work, not just over the next few years, but over what is likely to be many decades, possibly generations? The short answer: with difficulty. The longer answer: by being ambitiously pragmatic. We need to accept that we share our planet and interact with one another too profoundly to avoid cooperation, however much we may dislike one another. What we must do is define and internalise the fundamental interests that unite us."[104] How can we achieve what the columnist exhorts us to do? How can we be "ambitiously pragmatic"? What does "ambitious pragmatism" look like?

The first critical step is to overturn the dominant narrative. For centuries, if not millennia, most of our societies have functioned on the premise that a man is a wolf to another man (the Roman poet and playwright Plautus said it in the third century before

Christ: "*Homo homini lupus*"). In the 17th century, the British philosopher Hobbes popularized the idea that, in the state of nature, it's "every man for himself". This predicate may be stronger in Western societies that have a long tradition of individualism, but the narrative that we fight for ourselves and must disregard the needs of others (with exceptions of course) is rampant everywhere, and the more so the more one climbs the social ladder. It's not fortuitous that many participants in the financial market industry joke that, "If you want a friend, hire a dog." But such narratives are false, and the truth is something quite different: we are social animals "by nature" – an observation now backed up by science. As the philosopher and neuroscientist Patricia Churchland shared with us:

> In the last 10 or 15 years, the thing that has captured my attention has been neurobiology and evolutionary biology showing that, for all mammalian and bird species, we are social by nature (...). Over the last 15 years, social neuroscience has developed to allow us to understand the nature of the wiring that supports this intense sociality, particularly in humans, and in all mammals (...). People manage to do things that involve deferring gratification over many years, or they manage to do things where they act against their own interest to help a family member, friend or sometimes a stranger. We know there's also a tremendous capacity for self-control, and the cortex

> is very important for that. So, I think that's part of the story (…) Attachment, sociality, the need to be with others – it's evolutionarily deep.

Not only are we social by nature, but we also "have a preference for cooperative warm-hearted non-violent interactions compared to those that are selfish, aggressive and violent."[105]

Sociality is innate and starts at a very young age (the rudiments of empathy, sympathy and prosocial behaviour exist in very young children)[106] but, in her research, Churchland shows the vital importance of love and affection to nurture it. Some experiments conducted with rats and mice suggest that if some of the baby mice are separated every day from the mother for just a few hours, during which they are warm and fed, but don't get licked or groomed (i.e. loved), a change in their social behaviour and a reduction in the receptors for oxytocin becomes noticeable when they are returned. Then, when the females who were experimented on grow up and have babies, they become bad mothers, not really caring about their babies. So, Churchland concludes, "We know there are very particular aspects of the neurobiology of the circuitry that affect what kind of social person you're going to be and, in the case of mice and all mammals, it has something to do with how you're treated, handled and loved as an infant and as a child."

The research conducted by Churchland and other academics is proof that, contrary to the still dominant narrative, most people do care about others and about social welfare (not only about their own economic welfare). This emerging narrative is most helpful because it shows that this capacity to care – a prerequisite for successful collaboration – is contingent upon sentiments, qualities and emotions that can be encouraged, promoted and even taught. Love and affection, while possessing a social dimension, are deeply personal and hard to emulate at the societal level, but other qualities can be more easily harnessed for social good. Empathy (the ability to understand and share the feelings of another) is one of them. From an evolutionary standpoint, it is a quality that helps us survive in social groups and, according to Helen Riess, a professor of psychiatry at Harvard Medical School and the director of the Empathy and Relational Science Program at Massachusetts General Hospital in Boston, it plays an important role in our societies' ability to function, promoting a "sharing of experiences, needs, and desires between individuals".[107] Conversely, since our neural networks are set up to interact with the neural networks of others in order to perceive their emotions and to differentiate them from our own, a lack of empathy makes it much harder to live with one another without constantly fighting or feeling threatened by others. In short: empathy favours collaboration while the lack of it fosters fear and does the opposite.

Why, then, not teach empathy around the world? Why not train leaders and the population as a whole to become more empathetic? The examples of Denmark and Finland, two countries that every year rank among the highest in the world in terms of subjective well-being,[103] show that empathy taught in school from a very young age tends to reduce bullying, increases the capacity to forgive, and greatly improves relationships and social connectedness both in childhood and adulthood.[109] As empathy enhances the quality of meaningful relationships, it also favours people's ability to engage in successful forms of collaboration. By contrast, leaders who exhibit narcissistic traits (the opposite of empathy) believe they can operate alone and therefore don't seek to cooperate. Numerous examples in recent years have proven this to be the case, and the lesson is that, by focusing on actively teaching prosocial behaviour and qualities to children and students, countries will not only have happier people, but more cooperative and collaborative global citizens. This impulse is dormant in many nations, but why not give it a try at the global level and thus emulate the success of the few countries that have proven that it works? This is not a sentimental wishy-washy idea, but one that is grounded in science. A growing body of research, notably in neuroscience, shows that, "If you change your mind, you can change the world." That is almost the motto of the research Center for Healthy Minds set up by Professor Richard Davidson at the University of Wisconsin–Madison ("Change your mind, change the world" or "Change your brain, change the world"). Davidson has devoted most of his academic life to proving that cultivating positive qualities such as compassion and empathy can change our brain and enable enduring positive qualities to occur and to be expressed. "Through the embodiment of those qualities, we can set an example for others, and we know that one of the most powerful ways to learn these qualities is through social learning, and social learning occurs implicitly. So simply being around another person who exhibits these positive qualities, who radiates with these positive qualities, is an important ingredient in and of itself in promoting this positive change in others."[110]

There is little doubt that prosocial policies, if implemented at scale, would foster our collective ability to cooperate and, after a number of years, the results would start to percolate into society. But we don't have the luxury of those "years". The problems we face demand our immediate attention. We need to better cooperate globally now. What happens if we don't? Literature, as ever, can help us envisage what the options might be. At one extreme, we face a cataclysmic future devoid of almost any form of collaboration, like the one described in Cormac McCarthy's *The Road*, in which a few survivors cling to life in a nightmarish landscape. At the other extreme, we can imagine a world in which human beings eventually come together to find solutions. This is what Kim Stanley Robinson describes in the conclusion of *The Ministry for the Future*. In his novel, prosocial behaviour and the willingness to collaborate on an unprecedented scale are triggered by the enormity of the challenge (climate change). This is yet another example that the greater the problem and the more severe the threat, the greater the urge to cooperate and find a solution.

Currently, there seems to be little chance (and it's diminishing) of a general agreement or global solidarity regarding the global challenges that we face. This may change as they worsen but, in the meantime, what is the best we can do? Martin Wolf is quite forthright in prescribing the medicine: "We have reached a point at which the alternative to rising above our limitations is catastrophe. If we are to enjoy peace, to prosper and to protect our planet, we must agree to disagree, while still cooperating. No reasonable alternative exists."[111]

Humanity's immediate concern is to define and then implement a minimum cooperative framework that can address the most pressing challenges we face, most notably climate change and environmental degradation. This requires a deep level of engagement between the key players: first and foremost, China and the US. There is no reason the two giants could not act together to protect our global commons by defining a workable minimum level of cooperation. It would set an example that other countries could and would then follow. This won't prove easy, but it is incumbent on the rest of the world to remind the two superpowers that failing to do so would amount to a catastrophe imperilling the planet (and with it any hope of peace and prosperity). Put in the simplest possible terms: China and the US abandoning efforts to improve global cooperation would be pure folly

In practical terms, what can get us there? What cooperation narratives can instil hope about the way forward? Many tangible suggestions are being made, often evolving around the idea that centralized and hierarchical solutions will not work in today's fragmented geopolitical landscape. Instead, they recommend systems of global governance that are polycentric (having more than one centre) and multiscale (operating over different levels), arguing that only these will be accepted and effective. Discussing the merits of such broad proposals and "grand" narratives goes beyond the scope of this book, but an idea expressed by two of our interviewees could serve as a prelude for a positive and hopeful narrative on cooperation. It consists in starting small and local, and emphasizes the importance of "belonging" as a conduit for effective cooperation. Churchland argues that:

> It may be that the big changes won't come from highly coordinated policy across all countries, but from people recognizing their own local situation and how to remedy that, which then plays into the larger scheme of things. It's very practical and quite local. The locality part of the story is very important. Robin Dunbar, the British social psychologist, observed that we can only really know about 150 people (and we really don't know all of those), but they are acquaintances in some significant sense. That means we can't be pals with everybody on the planet. We must shift from thinking that we're acting on behalf of all the people on the planet to thinking that we can cooperate to achieve a certain common, practical end.

Along the same lines, but in an expanded fashion, Raghuram Rajan, suggests promoting the notion of "inclusive localism", which consists in "strengthening and empowering communities". An effective framework of global cooperation won't function without the buy-in of those who currently do not feel included in the process, meaning that global governance must coexist with local power in a way that makes it inclusive. Rajan explains it in quite some detail:

> To simplify, we have three pillars: the governments or political side, the economics, and the third or forgotten pillar, the community or social side. When the three are in balance, we get harmonious progress and well-being. When one or the other gets too strong, it creates imbalance and reactions result, sometimes from the other pillars, or society becomes dysfunctional (…) If we're to get balance back, we must focus on strengthening and empowering communities, on more decentralization and on more economic power, because many of the disadvantaged communities don't have the ability to work for their people and put them back on track" (…) "To the extent [the people] can determine things locally, they should, because that's what democracy is about. The globalization of markets means globalization of governance, and much less power locally. That creates populist backlash, but the kind of local determination that the local population wants often excludes a lot; they'll exclude global markets

> and become exclusionists, or they'll exclude immigrants, and it will be America for native-born Americans. What I have in mind is what I call "inclusive localism": more local power but used in a way that's inclusive. Borders encircle your local community but they're porous borders. They ensure we have a sense of belonging, that we're not uniform with people outside, yet they're not so high that anybody is kept out. Anybody who wants to join can come in. That kind of inclusive localism is seen increasingly in big cities and in some countries like Canada, where they're attempting to forge a sense of commonality among people. In the long run, it would be more empowerment locally, but also a community that's broadly accepting of differences. That's how we'll be able to deal with some of these broader forces like globalization.

The word "inclusivity" is key. The will to cooperate that underpins effective global governance won't happen without the greater involvement of civil society and local actors. UN Secretary-General António Guterres said as much in "Our Common Agenda".[112] He also sounded the alarm about the urgency of the task: "Humanity faces a stark and urgent choice: breakdown or breakthrough. The choices we make – or fail to make – today could result in further breakdown and a future of perpetual crises, or a breakthrough to a better, more sustainable, peaceful future for our people and planet." As expressed in various narratives related by our interviewees, the fact that we are confronting problems that are unique in scale, and that we are all in this together, may trigger a strong movement for global cooperation. We are social animals after all, and our innate proclivity to cooperate has the power to save us!

3.2. Imagination and innovation

Imagination, "a creation of the mind", but also the "ability to confront and deal with a problem",[113] is a glorious attribute. When its infinite possibilities are harnessed, it corresponds to a form of "superpower" from which every human being can benefit, individually or collectively. It's easy to understand why: every resolution of a problem begins with a bit of imagination. Conversely, many problems occur because of the failure to imagine that they could. The expression "failure of imagination" captures this by describing the expectation that future opportunities and risks will resemble those of the past. The novelist Graham Greene used it for the first time in *The Power and the Glory*,[114] but the 9/11 Commission made it popular by invoking it as the main reason why intelligence agencies had failed to anticipate the "unimaginable" events of that day. Ever since, the expression has been associated with situations in which strategic thinking and risk management are stuck in unimaginative and reactive thinking. Considering today's wide and interdependent array of risks, we can't afford to be unimaginative, even though, as the astrobiologist Caleb Scharf points out, we risk getting imprisoned in a dangerous cognitive lockdown because of the magnitude of the task: "Indeed, we humans do seem to struggle in general when too many new things are thrown at us at once. Especially when those things are outside of our normal purview. Like, well, weird viruses or new climate patterns (...). In the face of such things, we can simply go into a state of cognitive lockdown, flipping from one small piece of the problem to another and not quite building a cohesive whole."[115]

Imagination is precisely what is required to escape a state of "cognitive lockdown" and to build a "cohesive whole". It gives us the capacity to dream up innovative solutions to successfully address the multitude of risks that confront us. For decades now, we've been destabilizing the world, having failed to imagine the consequences of our actions on our societies and our biosphere, and the way in which they are connected. Now, following this failure and the stark realization of what it has entailed, we need to do just the opposite: rely on the power of imagination to get us out of the holes we've dug ourselves into. It is incumbent upon us to imagine the contours of a more equitable and sustainable world. Imagination being boundless, the variety of social, economic and political solutions is infinite. To find them, let's muster our collective capacity of imagination to elaborate a set of hopeful futures and map out the various pathways that would lead towards them.

With respect to the assertion that there are things we don't imagine to be socially or politically possible, a recent, much acclaimed book shows that nothing is preordained. We are in fact only bound by the power of our own imaginations. In *The Dawn of Everything,*[116] David Graeber and David Wengrow (a deceased anthropologist and an archaeologist) prove this by showing that every imaginable form of social and economic organization has existed from the very beginning of humankind. Over the past 300,000 years, we've pursued knowledge, experimentation, happiness, development, freedom and other human endeavours in myriad different ways. During these times that preceded our modern world, none of the arrangements that we devised to live together exhibited a single point of origin or an invariant pattern. Early societies were peaceful and violent, authoritarian and democratic, patriarchal and matriarchal, slaveholding and abolitionist, some moving between different types of organizations all the time, others not. Antique industrial cities were flourishing at the heart of empires while others existed in the absence of a sovereign entity. The point is this: prior to our "modernity" that culminated with the idea of the Enlightenment, there was an incredible variety of social possibilities that most modern people didn't imagine were possible. Rousseau's idealism about the "state of nature" in a pre-civilization world or Hobbes' conviction that life before the state existed was "nasty, brutish and short" look more like a hypothesis rather than the scientific canon they often incarnate. If ancient societies did not obey any specific organizational trajectory or evolutionary model, why should it be different in today's world? What prevents us imagining different pathways and new forms? What is it that constrains our ability to imagine better ways of dealing with our problems and why can't we organize ourselves differently? Are we not capable of creating entirely new narratives?

The answer is: yes, we are! For those who care to look around, new imaginative solutions to our global issues and collective action problems not only exist but abound. Drawing up an inventory of this immense panoply goes well beyond the scope of this book, so it will just offer a few significant examples to prove the point and enthusiastically demonstrate that imagination is not in short supply.

Every day everywhere, thousands and thousands of individuals are coming up with new, imaginative ideas and innovative solutions to address the problems we collectively face. Entrepreneurs, business executives, investors, policy-makers, social activists, academics and all sorts of other thinkers actively propose and experiment them. To communicate and thus deploy the power of imagination, nothing is more effective than the power of narratives, that is to say, developing stories that are both pertinent and convincing to others. This is the best way to motivate those with whom we interact socially, politically and economically, and to move the agenda forward. In our conversation, Carlota Perez offered such an example of a big narrative whose power of imagination leads to a call for action:

> Based on historical experience, we could see ahead a socially and environmentally sustainable golden age of the information and communications revo-

lution. It would require major institutional innovations, among them a supranational institution to regulate finance at the global level and several changes to modernize national governments, to devolve power to local levels and to redesign the welfare state and the tax system. All this would require aiming all policies towards smart (meaning digital), green, fair and global growth. I have identified a pattern that has been followed by previous technological revolutions (where the regularity is shaped by unique features each time): (1) A revolution comes together when the prevailing one shows signs of maturity and exhaustion (decreasing profitability due to market saturation and to the exhaustion of the innovation space to increase productivity or add new products, along the known trajectories). (2) The first decades (or installation period) are a turbulent process of 'creative destruction' when the new paradigm forces the replacement of the old. Along the way, new millionaires are made, many jobs and skills are destroyed, old industries are modernized or eliminated, inequality increases, financial bubbles rise and collapse. (3) The ensuing recession reveals the social consequences of the 'destruction' half. Protests, resentment, divisions and populism ensue, sounding the alarm bells requiring a new 'social contract', while also providing an understanding

> of the potential of the new technologies (the 'creative' half). (4) The following decades (or deployment period) can be a golden age if the state gears the potential towards providing such a contract, by tilting the playing field in clear directions, in order to get the most out of the technological potential and re-legitimize capitalism by making sure the wealth of the few benefits a much greater proportion of society. Such golden ages were, from 1850, the Victorian boom in the United Kingdom; from 1900, the Belle Époque in Europe (Progressive Era in the United States) and the post-war boom in the then-called Advanced West. In my view, the shift with the current revolution should have happened in the aftermath of the 2008 financial crisis. Having missed that opportunity, the pandemic may have (re)created the conditions for it.

This ebauche of a grand narrative shows that: (1) we can imagine a future that doesn't have to be bleak; (2) some of the challenges we face mirror previous historical epochs; (3) decisive action can help us move towards a more environmentally and socially sustainable world; (4) in transitioning to a new paradigm (that of information and communication technologies), we have to abandon the previous one (mass production).

The definition of imagination as "the ability to confront and deal with a problem" involves creativity and an openness to new ways of thinking, plus of course large amounts of disciplined analysis and the prospect of a business or policy application (otherwise, to paraphrase the Brazilian economist Carlos Braga's favourite expression, "vision or imagination without implementation is just hallucination"). Nowadays, all sorts of people are engaged in elaborating novel and imaginative ideas, products and strategies. They do so by developing new ventures, start-ups, economic policies or mammoth projects and, in so doing, create and shape the future. Their original ideas translate into narratives that produce models which in turn influence behaviour and help construct the future. Ultimately, they become instruments of policy and project market power. By way of demonstration, four innovative projects, or sets of projects, are described, all different from each other but all pertaining to the environmental sector (this macro category was chosen arbitrarily because it is where the stakes are the highest). Just a few years ago, all these ventures were unknown or in their infancy. Now, they are a collective testimony to the power of imagination of those who conceived them.

(1) Network for Greening the Financial System and beyond: Imagining new policies

The Network for Greening the Financial System (NGFS) is a group of 91 central banks and supervisors committed to mobilizing mainstream finance to support the transition towards a sustainable economy. It is investigating many bold financial innovations[117] that could (and most likely will) one day revolutionize the way in which climate-related risks are accounted for in central banking and banking supervision. In short, alongside governments (which have a much broader and more effective range of tools and policies available to prevent and mitigate climate-related risks), central banks will adapt their monetary policy operational frameworks to reflect climate-related risks. This will involve the mitigation of balance sheet risks that stem from climate change and environmental degradation, but also the active support of the transition to a non-carbon, green economy. Imagining what form this might take and devising policy tools and instruments to get there is the task of the NGFS, and largely depends on how climate risks will affect the economy and financial system through a range of different transmission channels.[118] The menu of options available is extensive and encompasses changes in all three most important policy fields of a central bank: credit operations, collateral policies and asset purchases. It is not the purpose of this book to delve into the technicalities of what this involves[119] but, suffice to say, some of the options represent a radical departure from standard central bank operational policies. They are, in short, the product of central bankers' imagination.

Some ideas go into uncharted territory, well beyond the scope of what the NGFS is devising in terms of possible policies. Creating "carbon quantitative easing" policies is one of them. It's a novel, untested and somewhat outlier narrative that already sounds familiar because it plays a key role in

Kim Stanley Robinson's bestseller *The Ministry for the Future*. In the novel, as the climate crisis gets dramatically worse, the world's top central bankers end up cooperating by collectively abandoning caution to the wind and deciding to create a global "carbon coin" to fund decarbonization. Robinson's inspiration is grounded on some academic papers published less than five years ago,[120] and lately on the work of the NGFS, that doesn't (yet?) venture into such wild territory. But asserting novelists' "poetic licence", Robinson's imagination runs wild:

> [The NGFS] suggested that possibly nations, companies and individuals who draw carbon from the atmosphere could be paid for it directly. Possibly petrostates could be compensated for the fossil fuels they keep in the ground. Possibly oil companies could be paid to suck carbon from the air and then pump it back into the ground; they could also be paid to pump water from under the great glaciers of Antarctica and Greenland, which are currently sliding into the sea on newly melted subterranean water slides. Of course, legislatures and citizens will need to urge their central banks, and ultimately to instruct or order them, to do these things. But the good news is that with these new strategies in hand, even in our current political economy, awkwardly suited at best to the task at hand, we might be able to pay ourselves to do

> the necessary things, and thus dodge the coming mass-extinction event.[121]

This idea is far-fetched, but it's already been picked by some hard-nosed investment bankers.[122] Besides, surely the very purpose of imagination is to venture into unknown territories!

(2) Nature-based solutions: An imaginative idea leading to a bloom of start-ups

It doesn't take much imagination to realize that nature gives freely. For centuries, not only have we taken this generosity for granted, but we've also exploited it to such an extent that we are now on the edge of a precipice. Of course, nature is not "free"; it is priceless, and a degree of imagination is needed to grasp what this means in terms of policy. For economists and policy-makers, valuing nature and assessing its contribution to our economies and societies is a recent endeavour because, for centuries, we've been overlooking the fundamental role nature plays in our lives and underestimating the risks that environmental degradation poses to human welfare and economic growth. Without taking care of the complex ecosystems that ensure that the temperatures remain tolerable, the air breathable and the water drinkable, we simply cannot function as societies. It follows that nature represents an indispensable input to economic activity. It is an asset. We need to treat it as such and in the process reconsider our measures of economic prosperity.

Recent economic studies conclude that more than half of the world's GDP depends on nature.[123] It renders services that are obvious (like fish stocks and bee pollination), and others that are much more difficult to comprehend (like the work of complex ecosystems within the soil that recycle nutrients, purify water and absorb atmospheric carbon). These are unfamiliar topics for economists and require, as just stated, a lot of imagination and disciplined analysis on their part to properly account for nature's contributions to economic growth. A spate of new articles and reports do this, incorporating natural capital for the first-time into a rigorous analysis of the sustainability of current rates of economic growth.[124] As stated in the Dasgupta Review:

> Collectively (...) we have failed to manage our global portfolio of assets sustainably. Estimates show that between 1992 and 2014, produced capital per person doubled, and human capital per person increased by about 13% globally, but the stock of natural capital per person declined by nearly 40%. Accumulating produced and human capital at the expense of natural capital is what economic growth and development has come to mean for many people. In other words, while humanity has prospered immensely in recent decades, the ways in which we have achieved such prosperity means that it has come at a devastating cost to Nature. Estimates of our total

> impact on Nature suggest that we would require 1.6 Earths to maintain the world's current living standards.[125]

In the wake of the imaginative research pursued by academics, entrepreneurs (followed by investors and business leaders) are starting to acknowledge the role of nature as an asset and transforming it into a prominent investment theme. Contrary to widespread assumptions and prejudices, they are showing that valuing natural capital and investing accordingly in it can generate jobs and growth. It should therefore come as no surprise that start-ups investing in nature-based solutions are proliferating at an incredibly fast pace – currently progressing at an exponential rate[126] and covering issues as diverse as the conservation of species, the protection of forests, the improvement of recycling and the reduction of air pollution, food waste and sewage pollution. The imagination of these start-up entrepreneurs seems boundless.

(3) The bioeconomy: Imagination fosters applications from synthetic biology

The bioeconomy stems from the above and is concerned about using nature (biological resources and ecosystems) in a more sustainable, efficient and integrated manner. This new "discipline" has been popular for over 15 years and described in various ways. In 2015, the first international summit dedicated to the bioeconomy defined it as the "knowledge-based production and utilization of biological resources, biological processes and principles to sustainably provide goods and services across all economic sectors".[127] Today it goes hand in hand with the notion of "circular economy" and finds applications in primary production like agriculture, forestry, fisheries and aquaculture and also in sectors of industry using biological resources, like food and beverage, pulp and paper, and parts of the chemical, biotechnological and energy industries.

Over the past few years, remarkable progress has been achieved in synthetic biology (addressed more specifically in section 3.7). Bioscience research is advancing at a furious pace, spearheading new bio-enabled applications in domains as different as agriculture, clean energy, health and industry at large. Entrepreneurs, venture capitalists and large companies relentlessly compete in terms of creative imagination to come up with solutions that, in a decade or so, might revolutionize our economies. The potential of synthetic biology is such that it's not inconceivable to portray a fully fledged bioeconomy that around 2035-2040 will use renewable biomass instead of petroleum to make the products that our modern societies require. All within sight are a new generation of plastics that degrade harmlessly in seawater and soil; biologically produced, carbon-neutral cement; alternative food protein sources that use less water and land and produce fewer GHG emissions; textiles and dyes whose production slashes carbon dioxide emissions and reduces toxic waste; and soil microbes that reduce fertilizer use, improve the health of soils, and remove carbon dioxide from the atmosphere.[128]

(4) Geoengineering: Bold imagination at work

Whether one approves of the idea or not, geoengineering (also called "climate engineering") is a feast of imagination. It consists in intervening deliberately and on a large scale in the Earth's climate system to alter or even repair the climate by reducing or reversing the processes that exacerbate climate change. This "mammoth" idea that would have seemed incongruous if not unimaginable just a few decades ago is now a serious – although radical –option to stave off a possible climate catastrophe. It has been popularized by scientists like David King who suggests refreezing the Arctic by covering the region with white clouds[129] or Gernot Wagner whose book (aptly entitled *The Gamble*[130]) proposes to reflect sunlight away from the Earth by injecting aerosols into the stratosphere.

Geoengineering involves consequential risks, ranging from air pollution to all sorts of unanticipated climate effects. It also poses exceedingly complex scientific, ethical and governance issues. Do humans have the right to deliberately change the climate? Who would have the authority to make the decision to geoengineer the climate? How would it be controlled and governed? Who would fund such a project? These fundamental questions remain unanswered but are under debate in academic and policy circles. This is again a tribute to humans' capacity "to deal with a problem" (the definition of imagination) and to devise innovative and unexpected solutions (albeit disputed by many). Geoengineering is not for tomorrow morning but, as the climate crisis worsens, such a radical and controversial approach will come up for serious consideration. When it does, the imaginative power of a small group of scientists will have paved the way for such a decision.

Fast-expanding knowledge lies at the heart of these four imaginative policies, ideas, products and projects. But they are also being propelled by an outburst of imagination spurred by the necessity to find a solution to the problems that beset us (in this case environmental problems). As Einstein pointed out, "Imagination is more important than knowledge. Knowledge is limited, but imagination encircles the world." The same applies to logic. "Logic will get you from A to B. Imagination will take you everywhere," he also said.

3.3. Morality and values

Morality is commonly defined as a set or system of beliefs and principles addressing right and wrong as they relate to behaviour and character. Values, by distinction, concern the moral principles and accepted standards of an individual or the social group to which they belong. The two, while distinct, are nonetheless intricately intertwined. To simplify (to the extreme): morality is more about cultural, social and other norms, while values are more about personal convictions and beliefs. But in the end, both help us judge what is important in life. They are the principles upon which we decide what is appropriate, and then act accordingly.

Today, the situation that we are collectively facing with its many challenges (as outlined in the book's first part) and pressure to find the best responses is prompting us to reconsider the role of morality and values in our lives and to re-evaluate how they affect our behaviour and decision-making. This has been reinforced by the pandemic, which, like all massive shocks, favours introspection. Confronted by a life-threating virus with our own fragility and immortality, interrogations on what is "truly" important to us as individuals, what matters to us as members of society, what key priorities should govern our actions, become more pertinent and spur us to reflect on many things to which we'd given little thought formerly. In our conversation, Amie Thomasson, a professor of Intellectual and Moral Philosophy, emphasized this point:

> [Because of the pandemic], there's been a prompt to reflect and to think about the kinds of values that drive our action. That comes, in part, from the interruption of our normal patterns of activity. (…) It's then that I think we stop being so complacent about the values guiding our action. We don't normally even notice them – we just go about our work, raising our kids, or whatever,

> without much thought. We're forced to react in times of crisis and have to rethink the values that are guiding our actions and rethink these kinds of basic normative questions about what our values have been and should be. It's analogous to what the philosopher Thomas Kuhn called the difference between normal and revolutionary science. In times of crisis, we're pushed out of our normal way of doing things, whether it's engaging in scientific inquiry or living in daily life, to stop and reflect on the kinds of values that guide our action.

The assertion that, in times of crisis, we cannot do things the way we normally do them and must reflect on the values that guide us is fundamental insofar as it may prompt us to act resolutely and to find, at last, the solutions required to make the world more resilient, equitable and sustainable. This is what the idea of *COVID-19: The Great Reset* was premised upon: change is always painful, so we should take advantage of the fact that we are at a critical juncture to implement the necessary measures that can redress most of the things that have gone wrong for so many years in the past. This requires a re-examination of the role of morality and values. How critical are they and how can they best inform our decisions and calls for action?

As most of the major problems we face are global in nature, it follows that they could best be dealt with if we are able to share some common values governing how this is to be done. But is this possible? David Krakauer thinks it's hard to devise specific systems that can foster coordination and consensus "when you cannot assume that we'll have shared values". Like several other interviewees, he pointed out that their absence is already "a given" in countries like the United States, where polarization is pulling people apart and fragmenting society. He offered, however, a suggestion: "We can learn from biology: How do complex ecosystems with many species that barely communicate and that have different objectives somehow live in a state of relative harmony? We must think of humanity in those ecological terms and start building institutions that can support diversity and not eliminate it."

Thus, welcoming a diversity of views, opinions and beliefs seems to be a precondition for effective cooperation, even when values do not necessarily converge. And they never entirely do. From a psychological perspective, and that of neuroscience, divergence is normal. According to Patricia Churchland, "Humans have always had divergence. Their neural circuitry is formed very early after birth in the context of the group they belong to, and their social values become very strong given that context. Consequently, it's very easy for groups with somewhat different takes on moral issues to feel that how they do it is right, and how others do it is not."[131]

Nowhere is this more apparent than at the international level, where there is so much misalignment between countries that promote various value systems, offering different models of political institutions, economic development, governance and social contracts. These value misalignments are not confined to geopolitical rivalry and have a tendency to spill over into other domains. To give just one example, provided by Rana Foroohar, which could impact the digital economy and the way it is governed globally: "The one world/two systems paradigm is real, and it's not going away. China has made it very clear that it's going its own way in terms of surveillance capitalism. There are no assumptions of privacy in China, and they're rolling out tech standards in the One Belt One Road system that may work well for China and for some other countries, but probably aren't aligned with liberal democratic values."[132] In such circumstances, where is a common value system to be found? It would be illusory to think there is one such system that would be acceptable to all, and therefore it might be better to acknowledge that different value systems can coexist and avoid one country attempting to impose its own system on the rest. One interviewee, Branko Milanovic, spoke for several when recommending such a solution:

> I think less imposition of one's own values on other countries and systems would make the world better because there would be less likelihood of a conflict. Many conflicts come from a certain conceit, particularly strong in the West after the end of communism, that the West's system is not only the best system, but the only one, and that everyone strives for it. That has already led to

> many disastrous interventions and, ultimately, to possibilities of a war because it could spill over into a conflict with China. One thing that's crucial for us all is world peace. Without peace nothing of what we have talked about before matters. But sometimes people forget that, especially if they themselves do not have to bear the consequences of wars but can cheer for bombers while sitting comfortably at home and taking children to school.[133]

Without debating the merits of this argument, it is worth noting that a growing number of non-Western thinkers and policymakers (including some of those interviewed for this book) express their impatience, if not their anger, at the "West" telling them what is best and trying to impose its values upon the rest of the world. Chandran Nair has made this point vehemently, denouncing Western arrogance (i.e. the belief in the superiority of its value system) and a "white saviour mentality whereby technologies and practices built in the West will save the supposedly underdeveloped, poorly governed and polluted non-Western world".[134]

No one system is perfect, and every country, region or culture defines its own set of values. In the early 1990s, the debate sparked by Singaporean Prime Minister Lee Kuan Yew about "Asian values" (centred on the cohesion of the community) versus "Western values" (centred on the primacy of the individual) showed as much. And yet, one all-encompassing value framework has been ratified by the 193 Members States of the United Nations: the Universal Declaration of Human Rights.[135] Its 30 articles detailing an individual's "basic rights and fundamental freedoms" and affirming their universal character as "inherent, inalienable and applicable to all human beings" form the bedrock of a universal value system. This book embraces humanistic values that unequivocally prioritize freedom, human dignity and a quest for the common good.

When value sets diverge, as they surely do, a possible remedy is to identify and concentrate on those particular values that coalesce around issues of vital interest to humanity as a whole, irrespective of culture, nationality and social norms. Environmental degradation and climate change, because they are truly global and represent such a massive threat to us all, could be the source of such a shared focal point. Wang Yi made this suggestion when affirming that, "We should stop blaming each other. We cannot be influenced by non-climate issues and use different values and ideologies to criticize other countries." Thomasson phrased it in a broader context:

> We must also ask a range of other philosophical questions, for example about how we ought to balance individual liberty versus social prosperity versus the needs of the climate and environment (...). And normative questions must be asked about what needs to be done about it and how

> we can balance those values against more familiar values of prosperity and human autonomy, among others. Then, we can engage in public discussions about the values and corresponding norms we ought to have so that policies aren't just justified by "Oh, this is good for my country," or by a power move that, "This is good for me and just try and stop me," or by "This is how we've always done things" or "This is how we do things here." Rather, it should be a discussion that requires a cross-cultural public justification of why we ought to uphold certain values and do things in a certain way, of what the values and norms ought to be. (…) The more interconnected we are, the more we need this discussion to be broad and to include all the stakeholders to think about what values we ought to have.[136]

Once enough people agree on a set of common values, we can then start working collectively to make the required changes.

This will only be effective if we place morality and values at the core of our lives and institutions, and this has to start with economics. The reason is straightforward: our greatest global challenges can only be addressed in a meaningful manner if the issues of morality and values are (re)introduced into the practice of economics and the policies that ensue. This was at the core of what "political economy" meant in the 19th century. "Giants" of economic thinking, like Adam Smith, put political choice at the heart of the discipline and reasoned as social philosophers – values were paramount in their thinking. Today, by contrast, they tend to be put aside by contemporary "rigorous" economic analysis as if they were an exogeneous attribute. Too often, economics resembles a mathematical abstraction, approached by its practitioners as if it were an engineering discipline charged with fixing the bits and pieces of the "system" that don't work properly. But essentially, economics is about values because it's about the choices we collectively make as society and, according to Diane Coyle, "It is a delusion to think the value judgments involved can be delegated to others – elected politicians, say – or to believe that the economic analysts can stand apart from the society they are analysing."[137] We regard fundamental economic notions such as efficiency and discount rates as technical issues when in fact we should think of them as value concepts because, "What you're trying to do in thinking about the efficiency of public policies is to see what will make things better for society, and that automatically makes you think about questions of distribution, who will benefit and who won't, and ethical choices."[138] The same can be said about the importance of values when calculating the discounting rates (the way in which economic models value future assets and lives compared with their value today) to account for the impact of climate change on future generations. Nicholas Stern put it bluntly: "Cavalier treatment of risk (…) means that models have been profoundly misleading. (…) The theory of discounting ha[s] not been related to its ethical foundations or allowed for the risk that global heating will make future generations poorer."[139] It is worth quoting him in full to support the argument that incorporating values is a necessity if we are to deal comprehensively and successfully with the complex and interlocking global challenges ahead of us:

> [New approaches to economics] should examine rapid changes in (endogenously determined) beliefs and preferences; and take into account distributive impacts and risks, both at a moment in time and over time, and including those associated with structural change. All of this will unavoidably involve explicit analysis and discussion of value judgements. These components, or sets of questions, are difficult to incorporate in standard integrated assessment modelling, but are at the core of the issues around understanding policy towards climate change. We must deepen our economic analysis to incorporate them. We should also recognise that questions embodied in, or similar to, these components arise in many other parts of economics, where major risks and fundamental change are at the core of the challenge under examination. Thus, the issues we are raising here on understanding policy towards major challenges concern economics as a whole, and not just the economics of climate change.[140]

What is true of values is equally true of morality: it cannot be excluded from economics and the decisions we make. The economic profession at large tends to disregard moral issues (which it leaves to moral philosophers and social scientists), but moral judgements constantly interfere with economics and the conduct of economic policies. Besides, morality is an important factor in individual behaviour and thus impacts economic outcomes. It can therefore "influence current economic performance".[141]

Slowly but surely, morality is entering economics via interdisciplinarity and insights from neuroscience, psychology and behavioural studies. As already mentioned, the mistaken single picture of the *homo economicus* as an optimizing "machine" is incomplete, at best. We now know that the fundamental concepts that underpin classical economics (like the maximization of interest, fixed preferences and rational decision-making) are either wrong or at least much too limiting. Yes, we human beings are selfish, delusional and short-sighted, but we are at the same time profoundly altruistic and attuned to the needs of others. We do care not only about our children and close family members and their future, but about other people and the future of the planet as well. Hence, morality and value considerations constantly interfere with our decisions, both individual and collective. The new disciplines of narrative economics, evolutionary economics and agent-based modelling are starting to take this into account. Their influence is growing but they remain embryonic. Concurrently, some "mainstream" economists are also drawing public attention to the need to not dissociate morality from economics. Luigi Zingales from the University of Chicago is one of them.[142]

His pioneering work on crony capitalism, regulatory capture and how the pernicious collusion between "big business" and "big government" operates, helps to understand the current resistance to some of the measures destined to tackle environmental degradation or the reduction in inequalities. When firms or industries fix the rules of the game in their favour, this amounts to a form of "legal" corruption that subverts competition, hinders the functioning of the markets and gives a very bad name to capitalism. Hence, only morality and the primacy of values can reinstate the search for the common good at the core of policy. Pointedly, Rebecca Henderson said:

> I spend time trying to persuade my colleagues in economics that not only is burning the planet bad for business, but also that it's fundamentally amoral in terms of economics itself. (…) Under certain assumptions, when markets are fully competitive and externalities are fully priced, maximizing profits can get us to the Pareto frontier; it could be an approximation of maximizing welfare. But when markets are not fully competitive and externalities are not fully priced – I can dump greenhouse gases for free causing massive harm to public health right now and cause harm for thousands of years to millions of people – that's not the market that economics had in mind. That was not the fundamental foundation. So, I spent a lot of time trying to use the basic tenets of economics

> to say that economics has always been moral. You thought you could abstract it and just do the mathematics but, if the market is failing this badly, then you have to think about the morality.[143]

How could it be otherwise? Companies and the economy in which they operate are human and social institutions. As a consequence and at every turn, decisions made about how we work, how we are remunerated, how healthy we are, how demands from the community are considered, and so on, entail moral considerations underpinned by specific value systems. The "simple" question of remuneration makes this obvious. Top American CEOs earn on average 351 times more than the "typical" worker. Is this merely a technical or governance issue left at the entire discretion of the company's remuneration committee, or should it also entail a moral dimension? Some professions, like investment banking, command considerable bonuses while others, like medicine, have none. A short seller can make millions in bonuses but a cardiac surgeon who may save your life makes none, nor will they expect a share of your future income when a life-saving operation is successful. Is this a fact-of-life simply to be accepted, or does it speak to our values? In conclusion, the innumerable business and economic decisions that are taken daily cannot be exempt from moral calls and value judgements.

In his book, *Value(s)*, Mark Carney argues that capitalism has fallen short of producing a fairer and more resilient world because of the systemic misalignment between market values and human values.[144] Market values are about knowing the price of everything, except for the things that have no market price: human values. But we live in market societies (not simply in market economies)[145] in which the price of everything is becoming the value of everything. Hence, we become incapable of ascribing a particular value to moral qualities that are important for a well-functioning society.

Truly shared values and well-established moral principles such as integrity, solidarity and fairness are the glue that binds societies, enabling them to function and thrive in an atmosphere of trust. The magnitude of the issues we collectively face today (a deadly virus making us fear for our lives; the climate and environmental crisis and the degradation of nature generating existential fear about the future; the speed of technological change provoking anxiety for our livelihoods and way of life) often shifts our attitudes from altruistic to self-centred. Egoistic positions tend to deny the validity of any other opinion, which polarizes people. Today, this polarization is cleaving our liberal societies and is a key threat to their very survival. An effective response demands the re-establishment of trust, which in turn is only possible if political and business leaders exemplify the moral standards expected of them. Only by walking the value talk will they have the authority to implement essential value-oriented policies. And only then will these policies be capable of serving society and meeting the demands of our planetary boundaries.

3.4. Public policies

Of necessity, this section only touches on the broad contours of policy, leaving aside myriad details and nuances (which would have made this book much longer). Its purpose is simply to express some convictions about what ought to be done and share a few observations about upcoming policies. It begins with an assertion: policies must be sustainable because there is no other possible path conducive to social, economic and environmental welfare. In short, sustainability is the only feasible way forward.

But not every policy-maker, voter or citizen shares this conviction. Many still question whether we might be moving too fast (or even whether we should be moving at all) towards a decarbonized economy. In addition, certain businesses, industries, regions and even countries have a vested interest in slowing down the move towards sustainability. Yet, the science is incontrovertible. As the IPCC and cohorts of scientists have shown, not moving right away and decisively would render our biosphere so hostile as to derail global economic growth and undermine our living standards, further endangering political and social stability.

If the science is incontrovertible, so is, in a way, common sense. It's hard to comprehend how the move towards environmental sustainability could take place without a concomitant move towards social sustainability. Being intimately intertwined, the two must go hand in hand. As shown in section 2.4, in many countries around the world the social fabric that binds societies together is fraying, giving rise to mistrust, angst, sometimes anger, and a pervasive sense of dissatisfaction and uneasiness. This, in turn, leads to polarization and populism. Leaving moral considerations aside, populism tends to be bad for sustainability: first, a strong correlation exists between populism and climate scepticism;[146] second, populism brings demagogues to power, who then offer oversimplified and unworkable solutions to complex problems (environmental policies being one of them). In addition, they erode social capital still further. In fact, climate policy is social policy, possibly even more so in developing countries than in the rich world. The poorest communities tend to be the most affected by global warming while they have the least resources to cope with the climate crisis. For this reason, countries like Pakistan place the twin objectives of social welfare and climate action at the heart of their long-term legislative agenda.[147]

Sustainability is normally defined as the ability to meet our own needs without compromising the ability of future generations to meet theirs. It amounts to asking ourselves what we should leave to the next generations to ensure that they have opportunities at least as good as those of the previous generation. What assets do we want to pass on to them? Physical capital (infrastructure, buildings, machinery) comes naturally to mind, as does natural capital (our ecosystems: water, air, land, forests, biodiversity and oceans), human capital (health and education) and social capital (public trust, strong institutions and social cohesion). All four forms of capital are essential, but the viable development of future generations depends critically on the quality of natural, human and social capital which, too often, tend to be regarded as not equally important or relevant.[148] Herein lies the vital necessity of sustainability. Environmental sustainability preserves natural capital while social sustainability maintains the quality of human and social capital.

Taking this into consideration, two fundamental objectives should guide a common sustainability agenda. The first is to achieve the Sustainable Development Goals (SDGs) adopted in 2015 by all UN Member States. The 17 goals recognize that ending poverty and other deprivations goes hand in hand with strategies that improve health and education, reduce inequality and spur economic growth – all while tackling climate change and working to preserve our oceans and forests.[149] The second is to abide by the Paris Agreement on climate change (signed by 190 countries) and thus reduce GHG emissions to meet the goal of keeping the rise in mean global temperature to below 2°C above pre-industrial levels.

The policy imperative (and challenge) consists in delivering this combined agenda as rapidly and efficiently as possible. For reasons expanded on in the Introduction, a good narrative that can inspire the greatest possible number of people matters significantly. Currently, too many negative stories evolve around the idea that green growth (growing economically in an environmentally sustainable manner) "won't work", "isn't possible", "is a contradiction in terms", or "amounts to having our cake and eating it too". A simple search on the web shows that these stories tend to dominate the narrative. In fact, combining economic growth (albeit a different form of growth) and environmental sustainability is eminently possible if we put in place the right policies. Positive narratives must accompany these changes to instil hope and override the negative ones that tell us we are in a dead end with no option but to de-grow (it is indeed an option, but one that would entail catastrophic social and political consequences) or to accept our fate – having given up hope (that is, for the future generations). During our interview, Johan Rockström elaborated one such great narrative:

> It's almost a schizophrenic moment right now. Never has there been a reason to be so concerned, but never has there been so much reason to see the potential of scalable transformations towards a sustainable, healthy and equitable future. Why is this? The reason is quite simple. We have more and more evidence across geographies and sectors that sustainability is no longer the old environmental issue about how much we're willing to pay to reduce damage. It's increasingly proven to be the path to success, the next step in modernity. It's not only about technology, but also about system design, circular models, security and displacement, migration and conflict resolution. Interestingly, sustainability is starting to prove itself to be the only way to have a profitable, equitable, job-creating competitive economy across

different sectors. The strong example of that today is the fight over the car industry, which is in a race for survival. It's not because they want to save the planet, but because they want to survive as companies. But the only way to survive as a company is to go sustainable. That's the only way Mercedes, Volvo, Toyota and the rest can see a future. Because electric mobility, fossil-fuel-free steel, circular work with rare-earth metals – that's the way to have a demand on the market. That's our biggest hope, that sustainability is basically the path for nations, companies, regions and communities to have a prosperous and equitable future. Just look at food: there's absolutely no way we can feed 10 billion people in the world of tomorrow without going sustainable. There's no path, there's no model that can show that that is possible. We'll crash in so many ways – fires, droughts, floods, disease. But it's also the sheer impossibility of continuing to degrade landscapes while hoping to preserve productive pollinators and the ability to deliver food. Sustainability has become the narrative for success; that's the most promising component of where we are. It's almost like a perfect action movie script: we're rushing towards a catastrophe, but we have an action hero who comes to provide humanity with scalable solutions very fast, because we all win by that.

The bottom line: profitability and sustainability are not antinomic. The "green" changes necessary across the whole economic system described in several parts of this book can be a story of growth – they constitute, in fact, the only possible story of growth because a long-run growth story that is carbon intensive doesn't exist anymore. Painted with an extremely broad brush, the green growth story is as follows: in an economic world still characterized by low real interest rates, the multiple and ambitious investments required to go green can stimulate employment and demand. As we move forward, our economies become emboldened by all sorts of innovations spurred by human ingenuity, discoveries and investment. We discover new ways of doing things in a more efficient and much cleaner way than in the past. We realize, for example, that it's possible to recreate cities in which we breathe and move more easily – in which we live better. "It is potentially a very attractive, different way of doing things, relative to past dirty models, with so many gains across the different dimensions of well-being," observed Nicholas Stern, adding, "But that does not mean that it is easy. It does mean that it is sensible, it does mean that it is attractive, and it is within our grasp. We have to change radically and, particularly, invest and innovate strongly to get there. That is the challenge."[150]

3.4.1. Environmental sustainability

This is exciting but the policy challenge is considerable. To get a sense of what it entails, it's worth considering the European Green Deal, one of the world's most ambitious policy efforts aimed at transforming the EU (i.e. the 27 countries that compose it) into a low-carbon economy without reducing economic prosperity and while improving citizens' well-being.[151] It is articulated around three key points: (1) no net emissions of GHG by 2050; (2) economic growth decoupled from resource use; and (3) no person and no place left behind (social sustainability). Ursula von der Leyen, the President of the European Commission, calls it "Europe's man on the moon moment".[152] The Green Deal is based on an extensive framework of legislation and regulation that sets clear targets to achieve a 50-55% cut in emissions by 2030 (compared with levels in 1990) and a EU-wide goal of net-zero carbon emissions by 2050. This extensive framework is complemented by a broad range of incentives destined to encourage the private sector to innovate and invest. Specific action plans exist in a multitude of areas with key goals like cutting waste, using more efficiently natural resources and halting species loss. The Green Deal makes it clear that almost every major industry within the European economy will have to be overhauled, from energy, transport and manufacturing to food, construction and tourism. The European Commission estimates that at least €1 trillion will be required to finance the plan and that annual investments of €260 billion will be needed to achieve its 2030 emissions targets.[153] Part of the cost will be borne by the private sector, with companies encouraged to invest in green through loan guarantees from the European Investment Bank (which has itself pledged to phase out loans to fossil fuel projects). In addition, the European Commission has committed to a €100 billion Just Transition Mechanism to retrain workers who lose their jobs in the decarbonization transition[154] (reskilling is a fundamental point upon which this section expands further).

Like the OECD,[155] the European Commission believes that the green transition will create employment and economic growth, arguing that investment in new high-tech industries will repay the cost of the changes. As stated by Ursula von der Leyen, "The European Green Deal is our new growth strategy – it is a strategy for growth that gives more back than it takes away."[156]

As always, the devil is in the details. In the EU countries like everywhere else, implementing policies that combine pro-growth priorities with the promotion of environmental sustainability entails myriad legislative and regulatory decisions as well as complex trade-offs. To provide just a few examples and to start with the big picture, a price on carbon emissions where none existed before will have to be set, either directly through taxes or indirectly through regulation (according to various studies, the cost of carbon must rise from roughly $10 a tonne globally now to $60 a tonne immediately, and $75 a tonne by 2030 to hit the Paris Agreement targets.[157] The IMF estimates an increase from $3 a tonne to $75 a tonne by 2030, while the Bank of England predicts an even larger jump.[158] In addition to a carbon tax, all sorts of other tax reform policies will need to include provisions that increase reliance on environmental taxes. Infrastructure policies will need to better reflect environmental externalities when selecting specific projects and reflect these in transport pricing. At the same time, policies will have to favour low-emission modes of transport. Phasing out agricultural subsidies that distort sustainable food production and trade will also be important, but politically sensitive and perilous. This last point illustrates the complexity of the trade-offs involved, particularly those between policies necessary to ensure environmental sustainability and those pertaining to inclusiveness and social equity. The reason why Europe emphasizes the "no person and no place left behind" principle in the Green New Deal is precisely because the necessity of higher environmental taxation or of the removal of fossil fuel subsidies (in other regions of the world) will adversely impact the most vulnerable households to a greater degree. Therefore protection measures for the less privileged members of society must be a critical component of the whole policy arsenal.

Can such an ambitious policy become reality? Yes, it can! Four concomitant reasons suggest that now is the right time to move quickly and at scale: (1) The pandemic has shown that governments have the bandwidth to move decisively when confronted with a major shock. Besides, low real interest rates enable major investment programmes to be launched (this, however, will be much more difficult to do in emerging markets). (2) Major and unprecedented technological innovation will spur new sustainability solutions while reducing the cost of the transition (as discussed in section 3.7). (3) The zeitgeist has changed, with an international understanding that procrastinating is no longer an option. Now is the time to act. (4) Youth activism is increasing and will accelerate the transition because young generations want the world to change and become more sustainable in a multifaceted way: environmentally and socially.[159]

However, this doesn't absolve us, as individuals, from making our own contribution to policies via behavioural change. Tackling climate change in earnest will require both the ambitious policy measures outline above and a radical change in our collective mindset. If we want to avoid a climate catastrophe, we must cut emissions at a much faster rate than committed to so far, at the country, industry, company and, of course, personal levels. This means we will have, as individuals, to consume, travel and eat differently, meaning in a much less carbon-intensive manner.

All these new policies will have to adjust to unprecedented constraints, particularly in less affluent countries. Chandran Nair made this point very clear, hinting at the increasing role of the state addressed below:

> I think the idea that, by 2050, 6 billion Asians can or should aspire to live like Europeans and Americans through a consumption, resource-intense model is essentially a big lie, and therefore we must redefine the notion of how those people, in a climate- or carbon-constrained world, have access to basic rights. I think that's a conundrum today. How do we deal with it? We can't deal with it through pious statements and market instru-

> ments, but with draconian rules. And those rules won't be provided by markets, but only by institutions of society, call it the state.[160]

3.4.2. Social sustainability

As the pandemic showed, acute crises contribute to strengthening the power of the state. During COVID, having a good government (a good health system, competent civil servants and sound policies) could make the difference between living and dying, or between surviving economically or not. The epidemiological crisis prompted a return of big government, which will not be reversed. Like for COVID, it is hard to imagine how an exogeneous crisis as acute as the nature and climate change emergency or the social crisis spurred by rising inequalities could be addressed with purely market-based solutions. As written in *COVID-19: The Great Reset*:

> Almost overnight, the coronavirus succeeded in altering perceptions about the complex and delicate balance between the private and public realms in favour of the latter. It has revealed that social insurance is efficient and that offloading an ever-greater deal of responsibilities (like health and education) to individuals and the markets may not always be in the best interest of society. In a surprising and sudden turnaround, the idea, which would have been an anathema just a few years ago, that gov-

> ernments can further the public good while runaway economies without supervision can wreak havoc on social welfare may become the norm. On the dial that measures the continuum between the government and the markets, the needle has decisively moved towards the former.

For the first time since Margaret Thatcher captured the zeitgeist of an era when declaring that "there is no such thing as society" (in 1987),[161] governments now have the upper hand. Everything that comes in the post-pandemic era will lead us to rethink the role of government. Rather than simply fixing market failures when they arise, they should, as suggested by the economist Mariana Mazzucato, "move towards actively shaping and creating markets that deliver sustainable and inclusive growth. They should also ensure that partnerships with business involving government funds are driven by public interest, not profit".[162] Looking to the future, governments will most likely, but with different degrees of intensity, decide that it's in the best interest of society to rewrite some of the rules of the game and permanently increase their role. As happened in the 1930s in the US when massive unemployment and economic insecurity were progressively addressed by a larger role for government, today a similar course of action is likely to characterize the foreseeable future, with governments playing an ever-greater part in the provision of services that underpin human and social capital. The specific form this will take will be context- and country-dependent, but the most salient points will be the same everywhere.

Social safety nets, health and employment insurance will be strengthened and, even in the countries that are the most "market-oriented", extended unemployment benefits, sick leave and many other social measures will be considered and sometimes implemented – seen as an important foundation to strengthen communities and therefore social capital (the lubricant that allows economies to function efficiently). In many countries, renewed trade union engagement will facilitate this process. As the next section will make plain, shareholder value will become a secondary consideration, bringing to the fore the primacy of stakeholder capitalism. In general, there will be more regulation covering domains as different as workers' safety or domestic sourcing for certain goods. Businesses will also be held to account on social and environmental fractures for which they will be expected to be part of the solution. As an add-on, governments will strongly encourage public-private partnerships so that private companies get more involved in the mitigation of global risks. Irrespective of the details and the specific form it will take, the role of the state will increase and, to varying degrees, business executives in all industries and all countries will have to adapt to greater government intervention. Research and development for global public goods, such as health, education (the two fundamental pillars of human capital) and climate change solutions, will be actively pursued. Taxation will increase, particularly for the most privileged, because governments will need to strengthen their resilience capabilities and will wish to invest more heavily in them. As advocated by Joseph Stiglitz: "The first priority is to (…) provide more funding for the public sector, especially for those parts of it that are designed to protect against the multitude of risks that a complex society faces, and to fund the advances in science and higher-quality education, on which our future prosperity depends. These are areas in which productive jobs – researchers, teachers and those who help run the institutions that support them – can be created quickly."[163]

The direction of travel is clear. In the US, President Biden's "Build Back Better" bill (reduced to $1.8 trillion) places the "Families Plan" and climate measures at the centrepiece of his domestic agenda and represents a major stepping stone to create a more equitable and sustainable society. In Europe, the welfare state has the reputation of being the most extensive and "generous" in the world but it might extend yet further. The level of protection varies by countries (which administer welfare policies), but the European Commission has launched a new €750 billion "COVID-19 recovery fund" comprising four pillars, two of which are destined to reduce social and territorial inequality, and to boost economic cohesion.[164] In Japan, Prime Minister Kishida's "new capitalism" (dubbed as "plain old socialism" by an opponent![165]) will bring the prevailing neoliberal approach to an end by placing special emphasis on income redistribution. The list goes on. In the rich world, the governments' willingness to invest in human and social capital and, in the process, increase the state's economic footprint will expand further, driven by the realization that they: (1) will improve economic and social welfare; and (2) represent the best insurance policy against the rise of populism. This latter point is essential because dissatisfaction and populism cannot simply be addressed by "throwing money at the problem". It is a systemic issue that requires an all-encompassing policy approach and possibly a redefinition of the role of government. In Raghuram Rajan's words, monetary accommodation (i.e. pumping liquidity in the financial system):

> [doesn't solve] the fundamental problem of disadvantaged communities in developed countries and the fundamental problem of underdevelopment in the developed world (...) The disadvantaged communities have a problem of development, not a problem of stimulus. They need to be able to have the right schooling and healthcare to compete in very competitive markets. That doesn't come from pumping more credit at low prices to them, but from figuring out how to build the infrastructure and the right schools, how to get monitoring of what's taught in schools so that it's high quality, so that everyone has access to the capabilities they need to compete. That's the structural problem that needs fixing, in the banlieue of Paris and the suburbs of the small cities of the US Midwest. And if we don't fix it, the constant angst, the populism, the attempt to close out the rest of the world will keep surfacing.[166]

The pre-eminence of the government's role in policy doesn't equate necessarily to the return of "big government" – the current dominant narrative. Many reasons suggest that government spending will increase in the coming years (as a share of GDP), but its function and role will also evolve.

Government spending will increase because citizens, particularly in the richest countries, have ever-greater expectations over time. In our modern, transparent (everything can be instantly compared), fast-paced world, we feel entitled to a cleaner environment, better healthcare, good education, higher pensions, improved infrastructure. In sum, as we grow richer, we expect constantly rising living standards. And we also expect governments to do something about environmental degradation and climate change. Governments, particularly those in countries that run democratic elections, therefore have no choice but to deliver as much as they can on these expectations. Some items will require vastly more government spending, like healthcare and pensions because of ageing, and education and reskilling because of the speed of technological change. Productivity is poised to accelerate, but the adjustment in skills will be difficult for those less qualified and low-wage occupations. Preparing workers to adapt and ensuring that benefits are distributed as equally as possible will require a major effort on the part of governments. The difference between "good governments" and "bad governments" will be measured by how fast they implement the transition to net zero while providing concomitantly a welfare policy that makes societies fairer and more prosperous. Nothing prevents the greater role of government accompanying the progress of humanity. The state doesn't have to be an impediment, it can be a facilitator.

It is for this reason that in the coming years, the purpose, role and function of the state will evolve. Mazzucato, whose "big idea" consists in "rethinking the state", has argued for years that we have to stop thinking of governments only as a "fixer". When we do this, "that's the kind of state we get, which is too little, too late, always in fixing mode, out of breath!" Instead, we need to rethink "public institutions, public sector, public value, public purpose and notions of the entrepreneurial state – so that we can have more guidance but also better partnerships with business".[167] Simply put, the state and business can be good and efficient partners, even more so if we think of governments as being "entrepreneurial". The conventional view in mainstream economics that governments cannot spark innovation and should only intervene is case of "market failure" is wrong. All around the world, examples abound of governments spurring innovation, creating new markets and playing an active entrepreneurial role. This is as true in Silicon Valley as it is in Israel.[168]

Will a strong state and a productive partnership with business be sufficient to deliver environmental and social sustainability? Yes, if expectations are managed. As already alluded to in several parts of this book, the best way to move forward is to do small things and work at the community level. Offering grand solutions invariably seems to disappoint, generating frustration. By contrast, working bottom-up, achieving incremental progress and innovation, celebrating our own achievements and emulating small victories appear to work the best. And aggregated small improvements yields a better whole.

In ambitious, overarching projects like the Green Deal, it is the "deal" that matters. The "green" is well understood, with every expert and policy-maker knowing exactly what needs to be done and how. But the "deal" is the tricky part. Selling it to everybody won't happen unless environmental and social sustainability progress in unison, underpinned by great narratives.

3.5. Resilience

The pandemic has magnified the importance of resilience: the ability to thrive in the face of adversity and to rebound from difficult circumstances. As we emerge into a post-COVID era, resilience has become a buzz word and a "must-have" quality. Understandably! Everybody wants to be more resilient – hence the mushrooming of hundreds of books (including a *Resilience for Dummies* published in 2021) and courses on how to overcome shocks in the best possible manner and thrive when confronted with duress. Individual, societal and economic resilience are all intertwined because resilience, like all good practice, begins at home with every one of us.

The pandemic has made us collectively much more aware of the importance of our own physical and mental well-being in the pursuit of greater resilience, and of the necessity to address the issue of resilience in a holistic manner. Social resilience is as important as personal resilience in the same way that planetary care is as important as personal care. We cannot be individually well in a world that is unwell, just as we cannot be individually resilient in a society that is not (being a lone resilient individual in a society that is falling apart will take us only as far as the realm of the survivalists). This functional equivalence between individual and societal resilience can be easily understood through an environmental lens. Personal care is important to build our own resilience, but it partly depends on things upon which we have limited or no control, like access to clean water, nutritious food and good air quality. Planetary care, by association, is key to build societal resilience, which depends on a range of policy measures like limiting environmental degradation, reducing carbon emissions and introducing nature-based solutions at scale. Principles like those of the stakeholder economy, green investment and the circular economy bridge the gap between individual and societal resilience: one reinforces the other.

The necessity to make our economies and societies more resilient will be a predominant preoccupation in the post-COVID era. Economist Markus Brunnermeier makes this point in his recently published book, *The Resilient Society*, going as far as arguing that, "resilience can serve as the guiding North Star for designing a post-COVID-19 society".[169] In his opinion, societies could better withstand all the global risks enumerated in part one (like the economic and financial crises, pandemics, extreme weather events, cyberattacks, supply chain bottlenecks, conflicts) by making resilience a higher priority. Recently, societies have displayed a tendency to manage such shocks by either trying to avoid them altogether or reactively implementing measures to contain them. Such an approach characterizes much of the policy response enacted at the height of the COVID crisis (like zero-COVID polices and cumbersome health protocols). It, however, makes more sense to build resilience by investing in mechanisms and policies that acknowledge the existence of shocks while helping societies and economies to bounce back from them (like the widespread vaccination campaigns). The logic is this: we should not avoid risks because it's only by taking them that societies achieve breakthroughs and go on to flourish. Conversely, a society that refuses to embrace risk becomes fragile. Therefore, in a somewhat paradoxical manner, "enduring a small crisis from time to time can be preferable to avoiding them at any cost. A crisis is an opportunity to make needed adjustments",[170] which in turn represents an opportunity to build more resilience.

As anyone familiar with the poem "The Oak and the Reed" knows, resilience differs from robustness. It doesn't equate to weathering a storm and then (painfully) recovering from it. In this 17th century allegory, the French poet Jean de La Fontaine compares the robustness of the oak with the apparent fragility of the reed. The oak is proud of its strength to withstand the wind and other forces of nature. It derides the lowly reed that grows beneath it swaying back and forth at every gust of wind. But at the end of the poem, the violence of the wind is such that the oak is uprooted whereas the reed, temporarily flattened, springs back. The line reads: "I bend but do not break." The lesson of this narrative is that the reed shows resilience in the face of adversity and survives. The oak has a robustness problem: it is strong but once a shock breaks it, the damage is irreversible. Once again this evokes the concept of tipping points. Without resilience, individuals, institutions and societies end up being like La Fontaine's oak: confronted with a risk that is either unforeseen or too hard to mitigate, reaching a tipping point from which they cannot recover or, at best, from which they can recuperate with great difficulty.

Solutions to build more resilience into our systems and societies do exist, and their policy implications are clearly delineated. Brunnermeier mentions several in his book. Some apply to systems, as is the case for global supply chains or the financial markets, others to societies and nations. For systems, creating more redundancy and buffers is an obvious solution to make them more resilient. Redundancy for supply chains and buffers like capital requirements for commercial banks or foreign exchange reserves for central banks make eminent sense. For societies and nations, protecting the most vulnerable among us may be one way to build up resiliency by preventing social negative externalities, and proving that the concept of resilience can be like "a compass for developing a social contract that benefits all people."[171]

At the time of writing this book in November 2021, the most widely discussed issue of how to build resilience relates to global supply chains. They currently tend to be intricate and difficult to manage, favouring efficiency over resilience. When they are optimized, as they were just prior to the pandemic, they amount to fragile complex systems in which cost-effectiveness wipes out the redundancy that could make them resilient. Then, when something unexpected happens, as it did in the summer and the fall of 2021 after demand surged, outstripping supply, cascading effects occur and the system breaks down, triggering bottlenecks and scarcity, with significant second-round effects (like inflation and unemployment in certain industries deprived of intermediate goods and spare parts). In response, "just-in-case" is beginning to replace "just-in-time". Systems that run on a just-in-time basis have proven to be lean and efficient but also overly complex and as such very vulnerable (complexity brings fragility, and often results in instability). Simplification is therefore the antidote, which should in turn generate more resilience. This means that the "global value chains" that represent roughly three-quarters of all global trade will inevitably decline. This won't happen overnight because supply chains are difficult to disentangle, but the direction of the trend is clear. Every business whose profitability is contingent upon the principle of the just-in-time global supply chain will have to rethink how it operates and probably sacrifice part of the idea of maximizing efficiency and profits for the sake of "supply security" and resilience. Resilience will therefore become the primary consideration for any business serious about hedging against potential disruption, be it due to individual suppliers, fluctuating trade policies, or domestic and foreign politics. In practice, this will force companies to diversify their supplier base, even at the cost of holding inventories and building in redundancy. It will also compel these companies to ensure that the same is true within their own supply chain: they will assess resilience along their entire supply chain, all the way down to their ultimate supplier and, possibly, even the suppliers of their suppliers. Building resilience has an associated price tag and costs of production will inevitably rise. This will be a game changer with profound macroeconomic consequences.

This need for greater resilience is becoming a policy priority that extends beyond the realm of business. The last G7, under the British presidency, made it a key objective, for which it even appointed a G7 Envoy on Economic Resilience.[172] Its report, published in October 2021, highlights the critical need to strengthen the global economy's resilience against future risks and shocks, whether they be acute (like the pandemic) or chronic (like extreme wealth and income polarization).[173] In sync with observations made earlier in this book about the absolute necessity for better global cooperation, the G7 report (portrayed as a new "Cornwall consensus" that will progressively replace the retreating "Washington consensus") takes stock of the momentous collective-action problems confronting us, and argues that only renewed international cooperation and coordination of enhanced state capacities – a new social contract underwritten by a new global consensus – can build the necessary resilience to prepare for the task ahead of tackling the escalating, interlocking crises.

The G7 report on economic resilience suggests a radical reorientation in how to think about economic development, advocating that we should move from measuring growth in terms of GDP (gross domestic product), GVA (gross value added) or financial returns to assessing success based on whether we can collectively achieve ambitious common goals, such as avoiding climate breakdown or vanquishing pandemics. The report, whose aim is to build resilience, makes seven key recommendations, three of which relate to critical global issues: (1) COVID-19; (2) the post-pandemic economic recovery; and (3) the climate breakdown. On COVID, it calls on the G7 to ensure global vaccine equity and to invest substantially in pandemic preparedness. Equitable access to innovations that benefit from large public investments and advance purchase commitments is considered a top priority, potentially requiring a new approach to intellectual property rights. Regarding the post-pandemic recovery, the report supports increased state investment and endorses Nicholas Stern's recommendation to increase this spending to 2% of GDP per year, thereby raising $1 trillion annually from now until 2030. But it's not merely about more money: public investment must be channelled through new contractual and institutional mechanisms that measure and incentivize the creation of long-term public value rather than short-term private profit. And for the climate crisis – the biggest challenge of all – the G7 report on economic resilience calls for a "CERN for climate technology" that would focus on decarbonizing the economy by pooling public and private investment into ambitious projects, like removing carbon dioxide from the atmosphere and creating zero-carbon solutions for such "hard-to-abate" industries as shipping, aviation, steel and cement. This new multilateral and interdisciplinary institution would act as a catalyst to make and shape new markets in renewable energy and circular production.

These recommendations coalesce with many others presented in this book that emanate from academics, experts and policy-makers, like the one on CERN for climate technology that echoes that of William Nordhaus on carbon removal research supported by state funding. A pattern emerges: going forward, the public and the private sectors will collaborate in a much tighter fashion and the role of the state as a guarantor of greater resilience will grow. As Diane Coyle told us when commenting on the issue of uncertainty and resilience: "If part of government's role is to provide, in some broad sense, social insurance to safeguard people in society against things they've got no control over themselves, then obviously the question of supply chain vulnerabilities or vulnerability to future pandemics has really become a pressing one."

Some of our interviewees went further, like Chandran Nair who coined the expression "Insured Resilience" (or IR 1.0), which is about understanding "what the most advanced creations of the human mind are going to be used for in the next 30 years.' For him, the fundamental question is whether we can rely on technology as a panacea for the myriad problems we face, or whether we use it to ensure that civilization possesses the resilience to cope with our global problems while delivering sustained moderate prosperity for all. He uses the example of India to illustrate his point: "600 million Indians don't have proper homes. We've got to solve that problem with the best industrial material science technology. Food is going to be a big issue: how are we going to use digital technology and big data to solve those problems rather than creating artificial meat and all those biotech innovations? That's a big issue of digital technology overreach, and to use those innovations to build back the basics – the insured resilience."

Resilience is now firmly on the policy agenda, with ambitious and sometimes radical ideas on how to foster it at both the economic and societal levels. This could even be an all-encompassing project. In our interview, Xue Lan argued for the creation of a "Global Resilience Council", akin to the UN Security Council, but designed to focus on the non-military challenges that beset our global community.

3.6. Role of business

The role of business in the economy and society has always been a topic of debate. If we accept the premise that the ultimate purpose of an economy is to deliver progress for society, it follows that the same applies to business. Companies operate in economies (to which they abundantly contribute: 72% of GDP in OECD countries)[174] but are also human constructs built around employees, customers, shareholders and local communities, and anchored in our natural ecosystems. It's therefore only reasonable that they should ultimately serve us.

The core of the debate evolves around the concept of "shareholder versus stakeholder value" (or "shareholder versus stakeholder capitalism" – the two are used interchangeably). Is the ultimate purpose of a company simply to produce value for its owners (shareholder value)? Or, rather, is it to create value for both its owners and also for its communities, customers, employees and suppliers (stakeholder value)? For decades, the principle of "shareholder primacy" prevailed, ensconced in the analysis of its most ardent worshipper – Milton Friedman. In 1970, before being awarded the Nobel Prize in Economics, Friedman wrote in a *New York Times* op-ed that, "there is one and only one social responsibility of business – to (…) increase its profits".[175] From the 1980s to the early 2000s, the principle of "shareholder primacy" was increasingly sacrosanct. It fitted perfectly with the zeitgeist of these decades: the relentless growth of the financial markets and what seemed to be an unending Wall Street boom, the financialization of the economy and the growing focus on quarterly reports, combined with the uncontested supremacy of neoliberal ideals. During these years, being concerned as a businessperson about society or the environment amounted, in Friedman's words, to "pure and unadulterated socialism". It is worth quoting Friedman in detail to understand what those with a different opinion were up against. An indistinct whiff of McCarthyism was still floating in the air:

> The businessmen believe that they are defending free enterprise when they declaim that business is not concerned 'merely' with profit but also with promoting desirable 'social' ends; that business has a 'social conscience' and takes seriously its responsibilities for providing employment, eliminating discrimination, avoiding pollution and whatever else may be the catchwords of the contemporary crop of reformers. In fact, they are – or would be if they or anyone else took them seriously – preaching pure and unadulterated socialism. Businessmen who talk this way are unwitting puppets of the intellectual forces that have been undermining the basis of a free society these past decades.[176]

Until the early 2000s, unfettered free markets and shareholder capitalism seemed to be the only way forward. For me, as one of the authors of this book (Klaus Schwab) who had elaborated the concept of "stakeholder capitalism" the same year as Friedman formulated its polar opposite, it felt like a David-and-Goliath type of situation. The idea had gained some momentum but being right historically "too" early was the functional equivalent of being wrong! In 1973, the participants gathered at the Annual Meeting of the World Economic Forum unanimously approved a code of ethics based on the stakeholder concept. It stated specifically that the management of a company "has to serve society. It must assume the role of a trustee of the material universe for future generations. It has to use the immaterial and material resources at its disposal in an optimal way. It has to continuously expand the frontiers of knowledge in management and technology. It has to guarantee that its enterprise pays appropriate taxes to the community in order to allow the community to fulfil its objectives. Management also has to make its own knowledge and experience available to the community."[177] From 1973 onwards, the fight for stakeholder responsibility was an uphill battle. During these years, many businesses and financial institutions celebrated the "virtue" of greed ("Greed is good")[178] and had no moral qualms that, in the 40 years following 1978, CEO compensation at the leading 350 US companies would rise by 940%, compared with a 12% rise for the average worker over the same period (a dramatic disconnect driven by the wrong assumption that paying executives more would yield "the best" performance).[179] For almost 50 years, the commonsense idea that a company is more than just an economic unit seemed incongruous. And affirming that a business should be seen as an essential "organism" that can greatly contribute to the livelihoods of people and societal well-being was an anathema that amounted to committing a political sin.

Then the zeitgeist changed. In the 2000s, as environmental degradation became a rising concern and economic inequities worsened, an increasing number of business leaders began to consider a narrow view of shareholder value as misguided. Sentiments evolved, and business executives became increasingly convinced that they had to play their part in solving the environmental and societal problems faced by humankind. The logic that a company cannot thrive in the long term in a suffering community or in a degraded environment started to take hold, but the idea that a company should simultaneously generate prosperity, serve society and take care of the planet took many more years to percolate. In 2019, the "official" turning point from shareholder to stakeholder value took place. In August of that year, the US Business Roundtable, a major American business organization, officially endorsed stakeholder capitalism. Jamie Dimon, the chairman of the US Business Roundtable (and the chairman and CEO of JPMorgan Chase) justified that decision by stating: "The American dream is alive, but fraying. Major employers are investing in their workers and communities because they know it is the only way to be successful over the long term. These modernized principles reflect the business community's unwavering commitment to continue to push for an economy that serves all Americans."[180] That decision corresponded to a radical break with the past since the organization had previously "enshrined [Friedman's] philosophy in a formal statement of corporate purpose".[181]

It thus took almost 50 years to vindicate the idea of "stakeholder capitalism" – that is, to acknowledge that the purpose of an economy is to serve society and to recognize that no business can succeed in the long term without serving its workers and communities. The World Economic Forum took the US Business Roundtable declaration as an opportunity to refresh the original Davos Manifesto and expand it by incorporating some of today's emerging issues. This resulted in the Davos Manifesto 2020.[182] It reiterates the fundamental importance of stakeholder responsibility, stating that the universal "purpose of a company is to engage all its stakeholders in shared and sustained value creation". It also highlights other important corporate principles: (1) to accept and support fair competition and a level playing field, and to have zero tolerance for corruption; (2) to consider a company's suppliers as true partners in value creation, and to integrate respect for human rights into the entire supply chain; (3) to act as a steward of the environmental and material universe for future generations, and to consciously protect our biosphere and champion a circular, shared and regenerative economy. In a nod to the ongoing Fourth Industrial Revolution and the technological changes engulfing us, it also adds new principles: (1) to ensure the safe, ethical and efficient use of data; (2) to foster continued employability through ongoing upskilling and reskilling; (3) to keep the digital ecosystem in which a company operates reliable and trustworthy; and (4) to make customers fully aware of the functionality of its products and services, including adverse implications or negative externalities.

Nowadays, business leaders no longer consider the improvement of stakeholder value as an option. For all the reasons expanded in other parts of this book, they know that there is no alternative way forward. That is the reason why, in the coming years, measuring ESG performance will be the gold-standard of business adherence to stakeholder value. Many businesses do not have an interest in making the world better, and some will be tempted to engage in green- or woke-washing, but they'll be forced to commit to ESG and, ultimately, all the commitments will be put to the test by government action and societal pressure.

Contrary to shareholder capitalism that always saw government as the source of all "evils",[183] stakeholder capitalism welcomes the idea of legislative action to define with precision the benchmarks for ESG reporting and performance. There is nothing wrong with governments creating the right incentives and issuing appropriate norms for responsible behaviour, particularly when they represent the choice expressed by citizens in free elections. This then gives them the authority to determine societal rules. In the same way that companies have an obligation to report their financial results (quarterly or annually, depending on the countries and whether they are listed or not), in the not-too-distant future they will have a similar obligation to report on ESG metrics. Several initiatives have been undertaken to determine the best way to achieve this. The "Stakeholder Capitalism Metrics" of the World Economic Forum is a major one.[184] They will converge towards a standardized ESG performance metrics that works across industries and countries and that is supported by global standard-setters. Such initiatives tend to be led by business, but a globally accepted system of sustainability reporting will be a concerted effort of business, governments, regulators, the official accounting community and voluntary standard-setters. In the end, governments will make the last call for setting the legal obligations, targets and incentives around ESG standards and performance proposed by business. They will also ensure that stakeholder value is compatible with a rigorously defined concept of "societal and planetary value".[185]

In parallel, societal pressure and rising activism will accelerate the pace at which companies embrace stakeholder value and will "force" the reluctant ones to convert to the cause. There is ample evidence that consumers increasingly favour products and services from companies that are more ESG compliant. Accordingly, CEOs now consider that "adopting sustainable practices is the new price of entry to compete".[186] This trend will amplify as Millennials and Gen Z acquire greater prominence in the workforce. The young generations continually hammer home the truth that they have a majority stake in what the future yields because environmental degradation, climate change and rising inequalities will have a disproportionate impact in their lifetimes (the latter already represents a major impediment in terms of accessing decent housing). In light of this, business adherence to ESG considerations will become increasingly relevant to sustainable value creation. The price of not doing so will just be too high in terms of the wrath of activists, both social and investors.[187]

The above doesn't mean that business should become involved in every social or environmental issue. However, it suggests that when a company has a "stake" and its actions can exert meaningful and positive change, it should. Since, as argued consistently through these pages, global challenges require a global and concerted response, why wouldn't business play its role? This now sounds obvious, but it may require going beyond mere stakeholder value. Behind the stakeholder concept lies a basic recognition that, in our interdependent world, global challenges cannot be resolved by any particular group alone. A collaborative effort between governments, civil society and business – the essence of public-private cooperation – is required. This means that stakeholder responsibility must be exercised both at the micro level (the corporate level) and macro level (globally). This idea of "global corporate citizenship" is ensconced in the work that the World Economic Forum has been pursuing for decades. As expressed in an article published in 2008, global corporate citizenship, "expresses the conviction that companies not only must be engaged with their stakeholders but are themselves stakeholders alongside government and civil society. International business leaders must fully commit to sustainable development and address paramount global challenges, including climate change, the provision of public healthcare, energy conversation, and the management of resources."[188]

The ultimate role of business in society remains to do business, but global corporate citizenship is an extension of the stakeholder concept. It involves the corporation acting as a stakeholder in global society, in conjunction with government and civil society, and it's a notion that can be considered as a long-term investment. Since companies depend on the natural and social ecosystem in which they operate, surely it is in their ultimate interest to look to the well-being of that same ecosystem when it is beset by so many problems.

In fact, it's more than an interest – it's an absolute necessity. "Companies today face an existential choice. Either they wholeheartedly embrace 'stakeholder capitalism' and subscribe to the responsibilities that come with it, by actively taking steps to meet social and environmental goals. Or they stick to an outdated 'shareholder capitalism' that prioritizes short-term profits over everything else – and wait for employees, clients and voters to force change on them from the outside."[189]

3.7. Technology's exponential progress

Our greatest hope of successfully addressing some of the most major challenges we face (notably in terms of environmental degradation and climate change, but also certain societal risks) is harboured in the stunning speed of today's scientific and technological progress.

Hope, and the possibility of optimism, stem from the following observation: we are at a juncture in history when new discoveries and new technologies do not follow linear growth rates but exponential ones, drastically accelerating innovation. Azeem Azhar makes this point incontrovertibly in *The Exponential Age*,[190] showing that Moore's law (which states that the power of a computer chip doubles every two years while costs remain constant) now applies to a broad range of other technologies as well. The power of digitization, dramatic advances in AI and soon in synthetic biology imply that progress in domains as different as solar cells, 3D or 4D manufacturing, electric cars, urban farming, genome editing, augmented reality or online business now follow an exponential growth rate (that is, they follow a fixed doubling time, showing ever greater increases or progress as time goes by). Peter Diamandis, a tech entrepreneur, investor and co-founder of the Singularity University believes that, "in the next 10 years, we're going to reinvent every industry" and "we'll experience more progress than in the past 100 years".[191] Such an accelerated rate of change will generate great benefits and significant challenges (as shown in section 2.6) in equal measure, but a sense of great optimism prevails – a sentiment expressed by all scientists whom we interviewed for this book. Michio Kaku went the furthest, affirming that, "by mid-century, we should have an operating fusion reactor, and a workable quantum computer entering the marketplace. Brain-net [when the human mind is merged with computers] will take a few decades to get off the ground, but investors are already jumping into it."[192]

The fact that we always tend to underestimate the pace at which technology progresses has profound implications in terms of how we mitigate global risks and how we make policy. Take the example of low carbon-emission technologies. For years we were told that replacing fossil fuels would be impossibly costly – an economic aberration because green energies were bound to remain over-expensive in the foreseeable future when compared to fossil fuels. This has proven to be wrong. Over the past decade or so, thanks to ever accelerating technology, green energy has evolved much more rapidly than previously thought possible. The result is the emergence of a broad range of low-emission technologies competing with fossil-fuel-based technologies without subsidies or a carbon price. In the power sector, low-carbon technologies are already competitive with fossil-fuel-based alternatives. In 2020, solar and wind were the least expensive forms of new power generation in countries representing more than 70% of global GDP.[193] The costs of renewable energy technologies will continue to decline, in turn reducing upfront capital costs through innovations in efficiency and economies of scale. Today, it is proven that capital costs for renewable electricity decrease much faster than those for conventional technologies, resulting in the fact that, as an example, many electric vehicle technologies are now close to being cost-competitive with their fossil-fuel counterparts. In short, at almost every juncture, the pace of advances in green tech and the associated reductions in cost have proven to occur much faster than experts and policy-makers expected. As a telling example, the rate at which the cost of solar photovoltaic (PV) would fall has consistently been underestimated.[194] Across the board, and due to rapid technological progress, the costs of the new, cleaner technologies are falling rapidly and will most likely continue to do so. Hence, and contrary to the cliché that green is expensive, robust academic research now shows that a decisive green transition (that is, one in which current growth rates in renewables continue for the next decade) could achieve almost all the emission reductions needed to match the ambition of the Paris Agreement. In addition, such a decisive transition would: (1) likely be much less expensive than continuing with the current fossil-fuel-based system; (2) provide a steady and secure flow of energy; (3) not require any reduction in energy reliability; and (4) not entail any reduction in economic growth.[195] There will be bumps along the way, as shown by the brutal increase in energy prices in the autumn of 2021 and important adjustment costs in the transition period. Globally, fossil fuels still represent 80% of the total energy mix, meaning that the transition from "brown" to "green" won't happen overnight. During this transition period, fossil-fuel technologies will also be made cleaner with carbon capture and storage (CCS), carbon capture, usage and storage (CCUS), direct air capture and other new technological developments. But in the end, there is no doubt that "predictable trends in renewables can help us achieve cheap, secure energy, a healthy economy, and a safer, greener world".[196]

Members of the Energy Transitions Commission (a global coalition of business leaders from the energy landscape) concur, committed as they are to reaching net-zero GHG emissions by 2050. Their analysis demonstrates that achieving this goal is technically and economically possible. It is technically possible because there is no source of GHG emissions for which one or several technological solutions (available or in development) have not already been identified; it is economically possible because it should cost less than 0.5% of global GDP by mid-century to run a zero-emissions economy. Meanwhile, investments required over the next three decades to build a "fully fledged" new climate economy should only amount to 1-1.5% of global GDP.[197]

It goes without saying that all this won't happen by miracle. It requires immediate, persistent and decisive collective action from policy-makers, industry leaders, investors and civil society. But technological innovation makes it possible. The flurry of entrepreneurship, new ventures and large-scale manufacturing and industrial inventions fostered by tech is changing the game in a fundamental way. This is key: if we consistently underestimate progress in renewable technology, it follows that we also consistently overestimate the economic cost of the transition to net zero. The example of the UK (which is most likely applicable to all other advanced economies as well) proves this has been the case. The Climate Change Committee (CCC), which produces estimates of the costs of transitioning to net zero, has consistently reduced them as the costs of clean technologies fell. The analysis it performed in 2020 suggested that the annualized resource cost of reducing GHG emissions to net zero would amount to approximately 0.5% of GDP in 2050, lower than the 2019 estimate that put the annual cost of meeting the net-zero 2050 target at 1-2% of GDP. Back in 2008, the CCC put the annual cost of meeting a much weaker target (reducing emissions by 80% by 2050 relative to 1990) at a similar 1-2% of GDP in 2050. Two years earlier (in 2006), *The Stern Review* estimated the costs for reducing emissions (globally) by 80% at 1-2% per annum (comparing 1990 and 2050). The target of 80% emissions matters because of the assumption that the last few percent would be the costliest. The bottom line: the UK's current estimates put the cost of transitioning to net-zero emissions by 2050 at around half of what they were just a year ago – a 100% notional improvement enabled by technological progress. Any possible further surprises concerning future costs will most likely be on the upside (i.e. less costs), the reason being that technological progress is not abating but forging ahead, thus enabling strong economies of scale in discovery and production.

Since electrification will drive decarbonization, electrifying as much as humanly possible is a prerequisite for transitioning to net zero. In December 2021, the International Energy Agency (IEA) announced that, "renewable electricity is accelerating faster than ever worldwide, supporting the emergence of the global energy economy".[198] According to the IEA, by 2026, "global renewable electricity capacity is forecast to rise more than 60% from 2020 levels to over 4,800 GW – equivalent to the current total global power capacity of fossil fuels and nuclear combined. Renewables are set to account for almost 95% of the increase in global power capacity through 2026, with solar PV alone providing more than half. The amount of renewable capacity added over the period of 2021 to 2026 is expected to be 50% higher than from 2015 to 2020."[199] This is a remarkable progression made possible by relentless scientific and technological progress that will accelerate even further when long duration energy storage (LDES) solutions are found. Promising technologies like iron flow batteries and hydrogen storage, among others, are being developed. When they become operational, scalable and cost efficient, the prospect of cheap, abundant green energy will cease to be a dream.

Many such innovations are at different stages in terms of their development – some in their infancy and others well advanced – but, as they progress, they amplify each other in a "fusion" of technologies. Aside from the speed and breadth of what goes on in various domains and subdomains, it is the harmonization and integration between so many different disciplines and discoveries that make the Fourth Industrial Revolution so unique. The coming convergence of the physical, digital and biological worlds (the defining feature of the Fourth Industrial Revolution)[200] means that tangible innovations resulting from the exploration of interdependencies between specific technologies are no longer science fiction. Today, for example, digital fabrication technologies can interact with the biological world. In an effort to find inspiration in nature and go green, some designers and architects are already "mixing" computational design, additive manufacturing, materials engineering and synthetic biology to pioneer a new symbiosis between microorganisms, our bodies, the products we consume and even the buildings we inhabit. In doing so, they are making (and "growing") objects that are continuously mutable and adaptable (hallmarks of the plant and animal kingdoms).[201]

*****

Progress is here, but it remains to be seen what the next "big thing" in technology will be. Where will it come from and how will it contribute to resolving some of the biggest risks we collectively face?

For all the multiple reasons already touched upon above, it's hard to tell. There is such a profusion of different technologies that enrich each other, and they each progress so fast, that it makes prognostics hazardous. Even the ubiquitous computer is on the cusp of radical change. In 2014, Erik Brynjolfsson and Andrew McAfee stated in *The Second Machine Age* that computers had become so dexterous that it was virtually impossible to predict their application a few years in the future.[202] Seven years later, computer scientists and investors are confident that quantum computing will become commercially available within the next 10-15 years, destined to revolutionize everything we do by processing information millions of times faster than today's classic computers.

But in the search for the proverbial next "big thing", synthetic biology (whose development will benefit hugely from concomitant developments in AI and quantum computing) is a prime candidate. As already alluded to in several parts of this book, it holds the promise of reprogramming biology to mass-produce cells for the benefit of our individual well-being and that of our planet. Fighting diseases, increasing food production and generating energy in a sustainable manner, cleaning water, "devouring" carbon dioxide from the atmosphere: all these become distinct possibilities as biology and engineering progressively come together. Such perspectives prompt some biologists to declare enthusiastically that, "the potential [of synthetic biology] is for civilization-scale flourishing, a world of abundance not scarcity, supporting a growing global population without destroying the planet".[203] In the meantime, ground-breaking inventions are taking place in specific domains, with the very tangible potential of exercising a positive impact on issues like climate change. CRISPR is one of them. Jennifer Doudna, a biochemist who has done pioneering work in CRISPR gene editing and who received the Nobel Prize in Chemistry in 2020, said in our interview:

> CRISPR is a technology that allows scientists to change the code of life in cells. We can manipulate individual genes or the switches that turn genes on and off, and we can now do that in any organism with precision. That's the CRISPR technology and the breakthrough there. How does it help us deal with problems like climate change? Well, imagine that we could help bacteria be much more effective at capturing carbon and storing it in the soil. They do this naturally, of course, but we now have the tools in hand to speed up effectively the process of evolution and make them do this kind of thing better, faster and in the time frame that will be beneficial for dealing with climate change (…). No doubt radical innovation is coming (…). I think over the next

> 5-10 years, this will become one of the major ways that human societies will be able to manage the challenge of excess carbon in the atmosphere.[204]

The field of synthetic biology is awash with capital and ideas, as proven by the International Genetically Engineered Machine (iGEM) Competition that gives students all over the world the opportunity to push the boundaries of synthetic biology by tackling everyday issues facing humanity.[205] Every year, 6,000 university students and multidisciplinary teams work together to design, build, test and measure a system of their own design using interchangeable biological parts and standard molecular biology techniques. The richness and diversity of their proposals presented at the annual jamboree open a whole world of seemingly infinite possibilities. The clearest sign of potential success is the amount of capital being invested in the field. In the first half of 2021, companies and start-ups in synthetic biology raised $9 billion worldwide (both in IPOs and from venture capitalists), more than the total amount raised in 2020 and an almost tenfold increase compared to 2015.[206] In addition, established companies are increasingly creating joint ventures or working in collaboration with synthetic biology firms and start-ups in a broad variety of industries. The company Impossible Foods uses synthetic biology to create its plant-based burgers. Lululemon, the athleisure company, is shifting from petrochemical-based nylon to bio-built fabrics. Tyre makers are exploring the use of bio-based alternatives for chemical polymers traditionally used to manufacture tyres. Cosmetics and fragrance companies increasingly rely on ingredients supplied by synthetic biology businesses. The list could go on!

This extraordinary perspective pertains to just one field: synthetic biology. What about the others? According to strategic consultancy McKinsey's Technology Council, 10 top tech trends are of particular interest to investors and technologists (the biorevolution is just one of them) and are likely to shape the tech landscape in the coming decade. Naturally, they are all intertwined and combinatorial in nature but, for the sake of clarity, they are listed as follows (in no particular order): (1) process automation and virtualization – robotics, the IoT and additive manufacturing (3D or 4D) combine to streamline routine tasks and improve operational efficiency; (2) the future of connectivity – 5G and the IoT enable faster connectivity. Far greater network availability changes the business landscape by enabling the digitization of manufacturing, decentralized energy delivery, remote patient monitoring and many other benefits; (3) distributed infrastructure – cloud and edge computing help businesses boost their speed and agility, reduce complexity and save costs; (4) next-generation computing – quantum (and neuro-morphing) computing helps find answers to problems that have bedevilled science and society for years. It also helps industries like chemicals and pharmaceuticals cut development time with simulations, accelerate autonomous vehicles with quantum AI, and so on; (5) applied AI – AI algorithms train machines to recognize patterns, helping computers make sense of real-world data. This makes human–machine interactions seamless; (6) the future of programming – the rise of Software 2.0 provides organizations with a far easier, more intuitive and iterative way to customize existing code and automate mundane programming tasks; (7) trust architecture – a set of technologies (like distributed ledger) and approaches provides structure for verifying the trustworthiness of devices, enabling, for example, more cost-efficient transactions between buyers and sellers; (8) the Bio Revolution – this allows the confluence of biology, computing, automation and AI; (9) next-generation materials – graphene, different nanomaterials and a range a smart lightweight materials enable new functionality and enhanced performance in industries like energy, health, manufacturing, pharma, semiconductors and transportation; and (10) the future of clean technologies – new systems for smart-energy distribution in the grid, energy-storage systems, carbon-neutral energy generation and fusion energy have broad applications in industries as varied as power, transportation, infrastructure and water.[207]

The incredible intermingling of so many different scientific advances, discoveries, innovations and their manifold practical applications in business foreshadows progress and gives cause for hope. Technology seems indeed capable of (radically?) reducing the risks of environmental degradation and climate change. It also harbours the potential of improving our health and even our societal well-being. As stated in a recent World Economic Forum report on positive AI economic futures, "As technology advances rapidly and relentlessly, the task of thinking through positive futures cannot wait."[208]

Once more, it is for us to figure out what future we want. We know for certain that tech is a big part of the solution to the problems that beset us. We now need to confront the challenges on the road to the solutions. Raghuram Rajan said it unambiguously "While technology can create problems and must be managed, it offers the possibility of solutions, and we need to figure out how to take up those solutions."[209]

4. Conclusion

To a considerable extent, the solutions we find and the decisions we take to make the world a better place – more resilient, more equitable and more sustainable – depend on our willingness to enact positive change. In turn, this propensity depends on our collective capability to develop a set of narratives that instil hope. Hope is vital because the loss of it means we accept our fate and give up on change. As Minister Gergawi expressed it during our meeting in Dubai, "A person without hope is a person without life," to which the philosopher Martin O'Neill added a collective dimension, "We owe it to one another not to give up hope, and to work on the basis that we can solve the problems we face because, if we do not do that, we thereby abandon each other, and thereby fail to live up to what we owe to our fellow human beings."

In such a context, what does positive change mean? Since the spirit of an age owes its origin to each and every one of us, how do our own feelings of optimism, pessimism or pragmatism relate to a collective sense of hope (or not) about the future? We put this question to all our interviewees when we asked them what they are optimistic about and how that could translate into a positive narrative.

People have a diverse understanding of what is meant by optimism and pessimism. Literally, optimism is the expectation of a good outcome while pessimism is the opposite. But it's also an attitude: being optimistic tends to be seen as a virtue and has a positive connotation, whereas being pessimistic has the opposite effect. The philosopher Amie Thomasson frames it as follows: "I'd think of someone as having an optimistic view of something if they expect it to get better, and a pessimistic view if they expect things to get worse. We think of somebody as an optimist if they tend to make those kinds of judgements, maybe even regardless of the actual facts. They tend to overestimate the positive potentiality, and pessimists tend to underestimate it, if you're applying it to a person instead of just a set of beliefs." But do we have a moral obligation to form an optimistic view of the future? O'Neill thinks so, as he told us in a conversation:

> Optimism might be a duty or a responsibility, whereas pessimism might seem like something of a luxury (…). But I think that the idea of optimism is an idea that's more about a practical orientation to the world, rather than a set of beliefs about how things will turn out. The idea, often attributed to Antonio Gramsci, of calling for "pessimism of the intellect, optimism of the will" seems to hit on this distinction perfectly.

> His idea is a powerful one: our practical orientation has to be active and hopeful, even if our assessment of the facts is a negative one. Our active, practical orientation to the world should not be hostage to our epistemic estimation of the likelihood of success (…). In any case, whether one speaks of "optimism of the will" or of social hope, I think it's not an epistemic attitude but a moral and political commitment. It comes not from our assessment of possibilities but from our orientation towards living on justifiable terms with each other, and to being fit ancestors for those who come after us.

Gayatri Chakravorty Spivak stated it bluntly: "I am optimistic because one needs to be optimistic in order to get things done."

Many of the global thinkers we interviewed for this book adhere to the first assertion of Gramsci's quote ("the pessimism of the intellect"), concerned about the state of the world and the enormity of the challenges we face. Helen Steward summed up this sentiment when saying: "I'm not very optimistic. I fear that we have left some things too late; we haven't acted as early as we should have, and so some negative consequences are now baked in and there's nothing we can do about them. I'm not sanguine in the least about the future – it will be very, very difficult". Several of her peers pointed out that they are more pessimistic now than they were a few years ago, like Anita Allen-Castellitto: "I've been extremely optimistic all my life (...) but, in the last three years, the combination of what's happening politically around the world regarding anti-democracy with what's happening with racism (...) is causing me to lose my optimism and to become part of the fearful majority – those people who feel what we have is fragile and could be lost." Ari Waldman echoed her sentiment: "It's difficult to be optimistic knowing how far we've fallen."

Does the data and the analysis drawn from it validate their pessimism? The public debate of where we stand, how far we've fallen and how much progress we've achieved was ignited about 10 years ago with the publication of books like *The Better Angels of Our Nature,*[210] *Enlightenment Now*[211] and *Factfulness.*[212] Among others, both Pinker and the Roslings made a vibrant plea that the main line of history is one of improvement and that today's world is richer, healthier and safer than it's ever been. This is correct: on most metrics, if we had to choose throughout history the best time to be alive, it would indeed still have to be today. It is true that we live longer than ever, safer than ever (the likelihood of violent death has never been lower) and richer than ever (over the last century, global GDP has surged, while extreme poverty has fallen dramatically). Other metrics corroborate this, and as the expression goes: "We never had it so good." Just a few examples to prove the point: childhood mortality has plummeted and more children than ever go to school; deaths from war and terrorism are today at a historical low; more people than ever have enough to eat (despite continued widespread food insecurity, the problem has now reversed: there are too many people eating too much); and fewer mothers than ever are dying in childbirth. All these hard facts prompted President Barack Obama to write in 2016 that, "Now is the greatest time to be alive"[213] and philosophers like Michel Serres and psychologists like Steven Pinker to deride our innate tendency to think that it was better before,[214] often inferring it is false to claim that things are getting worse.

Yet, it seems equally valid to argue that there is much that is not going in the right direction. The first part of this book highlighted this reality, with environmental degradation and climate change at the top of the list. Also, it is possible to acknowledge that most things have improved dramatically, and yet still worry about the way in which others are going. Inequality is such an example. Yes, the world is currently less unequal than it was in the Middle Ages, in the Renaissance or in the early industrial age, but this of little comfort to those who suffer on a daily basis from today's inequality. Furthermore, both the world and our relation to it are very different from in the past. Significantly, we are much more aware of the situation of others, and our expectations increase as we collectively get richer. Inequality (measured by the Gini coefficient or the share of total income going to the top 1%) may have decreased from some extreme levels observed in past centuries, but it is now for all to see and in quasi-real time (velocity at work). Transparency, globalization and connectivity make the issue of inequality starkly visible and its tolerance levels much lower than in the past, meaning that historic comparisons will only get us so far. Of course, data does matter but so, too, does our subjective experience of it. The US is proof of that.

Despite being one of the richest and economically most successful countries on earth, the self-reported happiness of its citizens has been declining for a while.[215] So, should we be optimistic or pessimistic about the state of the world today and our collective future? The answer should be qualified and requires nuance: some things are going well, while others are going badly, and some very badly indeed (like the climate). In the end, we can be optimistic about certain things and pessimistic about others. Also, it's possible to acknowledge that things have improved a lot but won't necessarily do so in the future. One could even go as far as to acknowledge that things have improved dramatically, and yet be more circumspect about the world's situation and the direction it is now going. In a conversation with Steven Pinker about optimism and pessimism, the historian Yuval Noah Harari notes that we must be "realistic" (others would say "pragmatic") about our current and future situation. Harari broadly agrees with Pinker, but also argues that the famous cognitive psychologist paints a somewhat incomplete picture: "Things for humans are better than ever (...) but things are still quite bad. And things can get much, much worse".[216] The specific challenges detailed in the opening section of this book make it hard to disagree. That notwithstanding, hope springs eternal and therein lies the possibility for action and solutions.

Where do our interviewees go to find their own particular source of hope? Where do they see some collective ability to change things for the better? What makes them optimistic? Their responses can be grouped in three main areas.

(1) The first relates to our innate human ingenuity, flexibility and adaptability. Most of the 50 global thinkers and public intellectuals we interviewed recognized that, though the problems are daunting, solutions exist, and that our species has the intellectual wherewithal to identify them. We are the problem, but we are also the solution and, as Sadhguru said, "I'm optimistic about human beings. While they're the only problem on the planet, we can turn them around because we're invested with a certain amount of intelligence." David Krakauer emphasized the limitless nature of our ability to react in a positive manner: "Human flexibility and adaptability, and the open-endedness of human intelligence, make me optimistic. They are kind of boundless." So did Hela Cheikhrouhou: "I'm optimistic about human beings' adaptability and creativity. At every stage of history, people thought we were heading for some sort of issue, such as that mechanization will destroy the ability to create jobs, or something else. We've shown our resilience as a species through innovation, adaptability, creativity (...). The human species created the environmental problem, but I trust we'll find it in us to resolve it." Proponents of this "optimism of the will" do not fall victims of an unreasonable, Panglossian form of optimism. Rather, they argue that with creative thinking and collective will, humanity will come up with solutions and find time to avert catastrophe. As stated by Justin Lin Yifu, "People always have the intention to improve."

(2) The second is the speed of innovation and the role of technology, which the pages of this book address abundantly.

Patricia Churchland linked it to the previous point: "Human ingenuity is more expansive than chimp ingenuity. For most of our time, Homo sapiens just had a few stone tools. I'm optimistic. Without going whole hog on technology, I think tech, especially information technology, has been a tremendous boon for many people." Moisés Naím concurred but qualified this judgement: "I'm optimistic about technology and science. How scientists behaved in the face of the pandemic was admirable and saved lives (in contrast, the politicians in the face of the pandemic just became politicians – some denied it, postponed it or tried to hide it), so an enthusiasm for scientists. Of course, scientists also need government, public-sector support, accountability, and supervision. But I'm enthused by the capacity of humans today to find technological fixes to very difficult problems." Amy Zalman summed it up by observing that, "Scientific advances are mind-bending right now."

(3) The third and last, but certainly not the least, concerns the role of the younger generation and its propensity for activism. As Helen Steward pointed out, "If there's hope, it will come from the young; that's where my optimism is based. Over history, there have been intergenerational shifts in thinking, culture and ideas such as we saw relatively recently in the 1960s. People growing up in that decade thought very differently from previous generations in ways that made enormous changes to the way we do and think about things." Diane Coyle made a similar observation:

> [I'm optimistic about] the young people – the real change of mindset with the current generation. Becoming more activist, and accepting that there are big societal challenges that, as individuals, they can't ignore. It's that commitment to society that has really changed, whether it's climate activism or something else. One might not agree with young people about everything, but I think their energy and commitment are the biggest causes for optimism. They're understandably angry because they've had a raw deal from the Baby Boomer generation. Anyone in their 20s now emerges from university with student debt; they can't get on to the housing ladder; they've got a much more insecure start to their career; and they're looking around them at the fraught politics, the tone of political discourse and what's happening to climate and biodiversity. I think it's energized them. That's a really good thing.

Carlota Perez thinks alike: "I'm optimistic about the young. They understand smart, green, fair and global growth. And they see a digital green lifestyle as their aspiration in a fairer world." As mentioned by Ilona Szabó de Carvalho, this sense of optimism about the young generation is premised on the hope and confidence that we "are already sensing [among them] the awakening of more active citizenship" and their understanding that "the best way to change the future is to act on it".

As stated in the introduction, the ultimate purpose of *The Great Narrative* is to lay the foundation for a call to action. The mix of creative thinking (of which the interviewees were an abundant source) and a shared resolve embodied in the various narratives are aimed at collectively inspiring us and indicating a way forward. But what about starting with ourselves? Changing ourselves first? Leo Tolstoy famously wrote, "Everyone thinks of changing the world, but no one thinks of changing himself."[217] Cynics may argue that taking personal action is trivial and a distraction, particularly when confronting a problem as immense as climate change and environmental degradation. But this is wrong – both morally and philosophically. It is precisely because the problems we collectively face are so considerable and seem so intractable that it is incumbent on each and every one of us, both as individuals and as community members, to do everything within our means to seek solutions to them. We are in an emergency, and this is the only fitting response. As the historian, thinker and activist Edward Everett Hale aptly said in 1871, "I am only one, but still I am one. I cannot do everything, but still I can do something. And because I cannot do everything, I will not refuse to do the something that I can do."[218] Tackling an issue that seems overwhelming begins with practicality – with every one of us acting and focusing on the things within our remit, like being empathetic towards our fellow human beings, reaching out to those in need, making the right decisions on how we engage with others, eat, shop, travel, vote, and more. We need a new awareness of our responsibilities and a willingness to face them. For this, we must be prepared to change ourselves at the micro level and to have enough selflessness to accept new policies (in the broadest possible sense of the word) at the macro level.

This amounts to a belief that things can improve, inspired by an open-ended yearning for a better future, fuelled by hope and potentially successful if vital actions ensue. Nelson Mandela summed up the potency of such a mindset: "It always seems impossible until it's done."[219]

5. Annex

List of foremost global thinkers and opinion-makers who contributed to *The Great Narrative* project

- Anita Allen-Castellitto, Henry R. Silverman Professor of Law and Professor of Philosophy; Vice-Provost (2013-2020), University of Pennsylvania, USA
- Margaret Chan, Founding Dean, Tsinghua Vanke School of Public Health, People's Republic of China; Emeritus Director-General, World Health Organization
- Hela Cheikhrouhou, Vice-President, Middle East and North Africa, International Finance Corporation, USA
- Patricia Churchland, Professor, Department of Philosophy, University of California, San Diego, USA
- Diane Coyle, Bennett Professor of Public Policy, University of Cambridge, UK
- Jennifer Doudna, Professor of Chemistry and of Molecular and Cell Biology, University of California, Berkeley, USA
- Niall Ferguson, Senior Fellow, Hoover Institution, Stanford University, USA

- Rana Foroohar, Global Business Columnist and Associate Editor, Financial Times, USA
- Mohammad Al Gergawi, Minister of Cabinet Affairs, UAE
- Marina Gorbis, Executive Director, Institute for the Future, USA
- Leonid Grinin, Senior Research Professor, HSE University, Russian Federation
- Anton Grinin, Research Fellow, Moscow State University, Russian Federation
- David Grinspoon, Astrobiologist, USA
- John Hagel, Author, USA
- Graham Harman, Professor of Philosophy, Southern California Institute of Architecture, USA
- Rebecca Henderson, John and Natty McArthur University Professor, Harvard University, USA
- Michio Kaku, Professor, City University of New York, USA
- David Krakauer, President and William H. Miller Professor of Complex Systems, Santa Fe Institute, USA
- Justin Lin Yifu, Dean, Institute of New Structural Economics, Peking University, Hong Kong SAR
- Lu Zhi, Executive Director, Centre for Nature and Society, Peking University, People's Republic of China
- Mariana Mazzucato, Professor, University College London, UK
- Jamie Metzl, Founder and Chair, OneShared.World, USA
- Branko Milanovic, Visiting Presidential Professor, Graduate Center, City University of New York, USA

- Dambisa Moyo, Global Economist, Co-Principal, Versaca Investments, USA
- Jun Murai, Distinguished Professor, Keio University, Japan
- Moisés Naím, Distinguished Fellow, Carnegie Endowment for International Peace, USA
- Chandran Nair, Founder and Chief Executive Officer, Global Institute for Tomorrow, Hong Kong SAR
- Martin O'Neill, Professor of Political Philosophy, University of York, UK
- Megan Palmer, Executive Director, Bio Policy & Leadership Initiatives, Department of Bioengineering, Stanford, USA
- Minxin Pei, Tom and Margot Pritzker '72 Professor of Government, Claremont McKenna College, USA
- Carlota Perez, Honorary Professor, Institute for Innovation and Public Purpose, University College London, UK
- Raghuram Rajan, Katherine Dusak Miller Distinguished Service Professor of Finance, University of Chicago Booth School of Business, USA
- Johan Rockström, Director, Potsdam Institute for Climate Impact Research, Germany
- Sadhguru, Founder, Isha Foundation, India
- Landry Signé, Managing Director and Professor, Thunderbird School of Global Management; Senior Fellow, Global Economy and Development Program and Africa Growth Initiative, Brookings Institution, USA

- David Sinclair, Director, International Longevity Centre, UK
- Peter Singer, Professor of Bioethics, Princeton University, USA
- Gayatri Chakravorty Spivak, Professor, Columbia University, USA
- John Steele, Publisher and Editorial Director, Nautilus, USA
- Helen Steward, Professor of Philosophy of Mind and Action, University of Leeds, UK
- Ilona Szabó de Carvalho, Co-Founder and President, Igarape Institute, Brazil
- Amie Thomasson, Professor of Intellectual and Moral Philosophy, Dartmouth College, USA
- Ari Waldman, Professor of Law and Computer Science, Northeastern University, USA
- Wang Yi, Vice-President, Institutes of Science and Development, Chinese Academy of Sciences; Vice-Chair, National Expert Panel on Climate Change, People's Republic of China
- Amy Webb, Chief Executive Officer, Future Today Institute; Professor of Strategic Foresight, NYU Stern School of Business, USA
- Xue Lan, Dean, Schwarzman College, Tsinghua University, People's Republic of China
- Shu Yamaguchi, Author and Public Speaker, Japan

- Shinya Yamanaka, Director and Professor, Center for iPS Cell Research and Application, Kyoto University, Japan
- Amy Zalman, Adjunct Professor, Georgetown University, USA

Acknowledgements

The authors would like to thank Mary Anne Malleret for her invaluable contribution to the manuscript and Hilde Schwab for being a voice of "social conscience". They would also like to thank Rachel Houchin at the Monthly Barometer for providing such efficient support with the interviews, and Fabienne Stassen, who edited the book with much rigour and a sharp eye for detail.

Thanks also go to the many colleagues at the World Economic Forum who advised on, read, reviewed, formatted, designed, published and promoted this book. They include colleagues in the San Francisco, New York, Geneva, Beijing and Tokyo offices, specializing in economics, environment, geopolitics, society, technology, industry issues and public policy. Special thanks go to Kelly Ommundsen and Jaci Eisenberg.

Last but certainly not least, the authors are most grateful to the 50 global thinkers and opinion-makers who gave precious time to engage in enriching conversations about *The Great Narrative*. Great appreciation and thanks also go to the Government of the

United Arab Emirates and, in particular, Minister Gergawi for hosting a two-day brainstorming session in Dubai in November 2021 with most of the 50 global thinkers and some of their peers.

Endnotes

1 Margaret Chan, in conversation with the authors.

2 Allan Brandt, a Harvard University professor quoted in: Gina Kolata, "Past Pandemics Remind Us Covid Will Be an Era, Not a Crisis That Fades", *The New York Times*, 14 October 2021 update, https://www.nytimes.com/2021/10/12/health/when-will-covid-end.html.

3 The work of the Global Risks Network at the World Economic Forum makes this plain: all risks (be they of an economic, environmental, geopolitical, societal or technological nature) affect each other through a web of complex interactions. For example, economic risks turn into political ones (like a rise in food inflation triggering social unrest), and environmental risks turn into geopolitical ones (like extreme weather events triggering uncontrolled migration and border conflicts). See *The Global Risks Report 2021*. Section 2.1 in this book elaborates on this fundamental point.

4 Various reports can be found on the Center for Countering Digital Hate website, https://www.counterhate.com.

5 Merriam-Webster dictionary, https://www.merriam-webster.com/dictionary/narrative.

6 Interview with John Hagel, and John Hagel, "Narratives Shape Our Emotions", John Hagel Category Archives: Narratives, 23 May 2021, https://www.johnhagel.com/category/narratives.

7 Robert Shiller, "Narrative Economics", NBER Working Paper Series, Working Paper 23075, 2017, https://www.nber.org/system/files/working_papers/w23075/w23075.pdf.

8 The academic literature on narratives is extremely rich. A compelling introduction on how stories shape our thoughts and memories and even change how we live our lives is provided in: Dan McAdams, *The Stories We Live By: Personal Myths and the Making of the Self*, Guilford Press, 1997. McAdams, a psychology professor who has spent much of his career studying stories, argues that storytelling is not just how we construct our identities, they are our identities.

9 See Maurice Kugler, "The Economics of Ideas: Paul Romer, former Berkeley Economics Professor, receives the 2018 Nobel Prize", University of California, Berkeley, 17 October 2018, https://www.econ.berkeley.edu/content/guest-post-economist-ideas-paul-romer-former-berkeley-economics-professor-receives-2018. Paul Romer is an economist whose essential contribution is the understanding that new ideas lie at the heart of economic growth and that their non-rival character gives rise to increasing returns to scale.

10 World Economic Forum, *The Global Risks Report 2021*, 16th Edition, 2021, https://www3.weforum.org/docs/WEF_The_Global_Risks_Report_2021.pdf.

11 Interview with Moisés Naím.

12 Herbert Simon, "The Architecture of Complexity", *Proceedings of the American Philosophical Society*, vol. 106, no. 6, 1962, pp. 467-482, https://www2.econ.iastate.edu/tesfatsi/ArchitectureOfComplexity.HSimon1962.pdf.

13 The reason is that we normally try to infer an interpretation of the world by identifying patterns (even when they don't exist, like in conspiracy theories), but the number of patterns grows much faster than the amount of content (information) we have at our disposal. Two simple mathematical formulas explain this: an arithmetic increase in the number of elements in a system (like bits of information) leads to a geometric increase in the number of potential links (between these bits of information) and to an exponential increase in the number of possible patterns. The number of potential links (L) that can be established between different elements (N) is derived from the following formula: L= N x (N-1)/2. The number of patterns (P) that can be established from different links (L) is derived from the following formula: P = 2 to the power of L. Therefore, if we consider just four elements (bits of information), we may form 6 links between them (4 x (4-1)/2) and 64 patterns (2 to the power of 6). The question then becomes: is there any complex (or even simple!) system in the world that does

not depend upon the consideration of more than four elements or variables? The answer is that there is not. So let's decide for the sake of realism to consider more than four variables, like 10. Ten elements will lead to the creation of 45 links and 3,500 billion patterns, a level of complexity that exceeds by a gigantic order of magnitude the cognitive capabilities of any human being. See Thierry Malleret, *Disequilibrium: A World Out of Kilter*, BookBaby, 1st Edition, 2012, https://www.barnesandnoble.com/w/disequilibrium-thierry-malleret/1113883823.

14 Interview with David Krakauer. Information on the work of the Santa Fe Institute is available at https://www.santafe.edu/about/overview.

15 Gilles Finchelstein was one of the first more than 10 years ago to use the expression in his 2011 book, *La Dictature de l'Urgence.*

16 This argument is developed by Azeem Azhar in *The Exponential Age: How Accelerating Technology Is Transforming Business, Politics and Society*, Diversion Books, 2021, https://www.amazon.com/Exponential-Age-Accelerating-Technology-Transforming/dp/1635769094/ref=zg_bs_10020719011_9?_encoding=UTF8&psc=1&refRID=FPS71NCG7R6JQT25MRKZ.

17 Wharton University of Pennsylvania, Risk Management and Decision Processes Center, "The Ostrich Paradox: Why We Underprepare for Disasters", Issue Brief, 2018, https://riskcenter.wharton.upenn.edu/wp-content/uploads/2019/03/Ostrich-Paradox-issue-brief.pdf.

18 William A. Wagenaar and Sabato D. Sagaria, "Misperception of exponential growth", *Perception & Psychophysics*, vol. 18, 1975, pp. 416–422, https://link.springer.com/article/10.3758/BF03204114.

19 Carmen Reinhardt, "This Time Is Truly Different", Project Syndicate, 23 March 2020, https://www.project-syndicate.org/commentary/covid19-crisis-has-no-economic-precedent-by-carmen-reinhart-2020-03.

20 In the short term, a trade-off exists between the restrictions imposed on our daily lives and economic activity but, in the long term, the idea that a government could choose between public health and a hit to economic growth is a myth. Prosperous societies are healthy societies.

21 For the relationship between inequality and growth, see Joseph Stiglitz, "Inequality and Economic Growth", 2016, https://www8.gsb.columbia.edu/faculty/jstiglitz/sites/jstiglitz/files/Inequality%20and%20Economic%20Growth_0.pdf.

22 John F. Kennedy Presidential Library and Museum, "Robert F. Kennedy: Remarks at the University of Kansas", 18 March 1968, https://www.jfklibrary.org/learn/about-jfk/the-kennedy-family/robert-f-kennedy/robert-f-kennedy-speeches/remarks-at-the-university-of-kansas-march-18-1968.

23 OECD Better Life Index, "What's the Better Life Index?", https://www.oecdbetterlifeindex.org/about/better-life-initiative.

24 This approach focuses on the stocks of assets and liabilities contained within balance sheets (instead of flows, like GDP). Its proponents argue that a One-Earth balance sheet that takes into consideration human and natural capital would enable the world to improve overall resource allocation, deliver public goods and ensure more inclusive development. See Andrew Sheng and Xiao Geng, "Building a One-Earth Balance Sheet", Project Syndicate, 30 November 2021, https://www.project-syndicate.org/commentary/one-earth-balance-sheet-support-inclusive-prosperity-and-climate-action-by-andrew-sheng-and-xiao-geng-2021-11?barrier=accesspaylog.

25 John F. Helliwell, et al., *World Happiness Report 2021*, Sustainable Development Solutions Network, 2021, https://worldhappiness.report/ed/2021.

26 Conversation with Shu Yamaguchi.

27 Services are very diverse, but overall tend to have weaker productivity levels and growth rates than manufacturing. As a result, a shift to services entails a moderate but persistent drag on productivity growth. However, this might change thanks to new technologies. See Stéphane Sorbe, Peter Gal and Valentine Millot, "Can productivity still grow in service-based economies? Literature overview and preliminary evidence from OECD countries", OECD, ECO/WKP(2018)79, 2018, https://www.oecd.org/officialdocuments/publicdisplaydocumentpdf/?cote=ECO/WKP(2018)79&docLanguage=En.

28 Conversation with Dambisa Moyo.

29 This is an extremely simplified presentation of the issue. Inflation will erode real debt burdens only if it raises nominal incomes faster than nominal interest rates. Also, in emerging markets with a large share of foreign-currency denominated debt, the depreciation that normally accompanies inflation will raise debt service burdens. See M. Ayhan Kose, Franziska Ohnsorge, Carmen Reinhart and Kenneth Rogoff, "Developing economy debt after the pandemic", VOXeu, 3 November 2021, https://voxeu.org/article/developing-economy-debt-after-pandemic.

30 Sebastian Mallaby, "The Age of Magic Money: Can Endless Spending Prevent Economic Calamity?", *Foreign Affairs*, July/August 2020, https://www.foreignaffairs.com/articles/united-states/2020-05-29/pandemic-financial-crisis.

31 Agustin Carstens, head of the Bank of International Settlements (BIS), dubbed as the central bank to the world's central banks, quoted in Marc Jones, "Uneven global recovery creates 'daunting challenges' for policymakers, BIS says", Reuters, 29 June 2021, https://www.reuters.com/business/uneven-global-recovery-creates-daunting-challenges-policymakers-bis-says-2021-06-29.

32 Sara Brown, "How to prepare for the AI productivity boom", MIT Management, 12 July 2021, https://mitsloan.mit.edu/ideas-made-to-matter/how-to-prepare-ai-productivity-boom.

33 Paul Krugman, *The Age of Diminished Expectations: U.S. Economic Policy in the 1990's*, MIT Press, 1990, https://www.amazon.com/Diminished-Expectations-Economic-Policy-1990s-dp-B000H571KA/dp/B000H571KA/ref=mt_other?_encoding=UTF8&me=&qid=1639585827.

34 Parag Khanna and Balaji Srinivasan, "Great Protocol Politics", *Foreign Policy*, 11 December 2021, https://foreignpolicy.com/2021/12/11/bitcoin-ethereum-cryptocurrency-web3-great-protocol-politics.

35 A collective action problem (also called a "social dilemma") defines a situation in which all individuals would be better off cooperating but fail to do so. Since the 17th century, philosophers have been interested in exploring this issue (without calling it "collective action"), but it is the political economist Mancur Olson who theorized it in 1965 in his book, *The Logic of Collective Action*. In it he argues that in the case of pure public goods that are both non-rival and non-excludable (climate change is one of them), one or several contributors would reduce their contribution to the public good as others contribute more.

36 United Nations Environment Programme, "Addendum to the Emissions Gap Report 2021", https://wedocs.unep.org/bitstream/handle/20.500.11822/37350/AddEGR21.pdf.

37 United Nations Environment Programme, *Emissions Gap Report 2021*, 2021, https://www.unep.org/resources/emissions-gap-report-2021.

38 Countries that ratified the Paris Agreement have submitted NDCs that present their national efforts to reach the Agreement's long-term temperature goal of limiting global warming to well below 2°C. NDCs thus represent a country's current ambition and target for reducing emissions nationally.

39 Climate Action Tracker, "Glasgow's 2030 credibility gap: net zero's lip service to climate action", 9 November 2021, https://climateactiontracker.org/publications/glasgows-2030-credibility-gap-net-zeros-lip-service-to-climate-action.

40 Leslie Hook, "Global warming of up to 2.7C by century's end forecast as COP26 pledges fall short", *Financial Times*, 9 November 2021, https://www.ft.com/content/b9a55763-f28a-46ad-b265-79db73efa658.

41 Tariq Fancy, "Tariq Fancy on the failure of green investing and the need for state action", *The Economist*, 4 November 2021, https://www.economist.com/by-invitation/2021/11/04/tariq-fancy-on-the-failure-of-green-investing-and-the-need-for-state-action.

42 *Nature* conducted an anonymous survey of the 233 living IPCC authors and received responses from 92 scientists, or about 40% of the group. A total of 60% of the respondents said they expect the world to warm by at least 3°C by the end of the century, compared with the conditions that existed before the Industrial Revolution. As many as 88% said they think global

warming constitutes a "crisis" and nearly as many said they expect to see the catastrophic results of climate change in their lifetime. See Jeff Tollefson, "Top climate scientists are sceptical that nations will rein in global warming", *Nature*, 1 November 2021, https://www.nature.com/articles/d41586-021-02990-w.

43 Intergovernmental Panel on Climate Change, "AR6 Climate Change 2021: The Physical Science Basis", 2021, https://www.ipcc.ch/report/ar6/wg1.

44 United Nations, "Climate and weather-related disasters surge five-fold over 50 years, but early warnings save lives - WMO report", UN News, 1 September 2021, https://news.un.org/en/story/2021/09/1098662.

45 This quote and the following are based on our conversation with Johan Rockström.

46 Energy Transitions Commission, "Keeping 1.5°C Alive: Closing the Gap in the 2020s", Executive Summary, 2021, https://www.energy-transitions.org/wp-content/uploads/2021/09/ETC-Keeping-1.5C-Alive-Closing-the-Gap-in-the-2020s-Executive-Summary.pdf.

47 Myles Allen, et al., *Special Report: Global Warming of 1.5°C, Summary for Policymakers*, Intergovernmental Panel on Climate Change, 2018, https://www.ipcc.ch/sr15/chapter/spm.

48 Economist William Nordhaus made them explicit in a keynote address delivered to G20 foreign ministers and central bank governors in

Venice in July 2021. See "Why Climate Policy Has Failed", *Foreign Affairs*, 12 October 2021, https://www.foreignaffairs.com/articles/world/2021-10-12/why-climate-policy-has-failed.

49 Ibid.

50 Tariq Fancy, "Tariq Fancy on the failure of green investing and the need for state action", *The Economist*, 4 November 2021.

51 Energy Transitions Commission, "Keeping 1.5°C Alive: Actions for the 2020s", 2021, https://www.energy-transitions.org/publications/keeping-1-5-alive.

52 Glasgow Financial Alliance for Net Zero (GFANZ), "Amount of finance committed to achieving 1.5°C now at scale needed to deliver the transition", 3 November 2021, https://www.gfanzero.com/press/amount-of-finance-committed-to-achieving-1-5c-now-at-scale-needed-to-deliver-the-transition.

53 Damian Carrington, "Climate crisis: economists 'grossly undervalue young lives', warns Stern", *The Guardian*, 25 October 2021, https://www.theguardian.com/environment/2021/oct/26/climate-crisis-economists-grossly-undervalue-young-lives-warns-stern.

54 Vitor Gaspar and Ian Parry, "A Proposal to Scale Up Global Carbon Pricing", International Monetary Fund, 18 June 2021, https://blogs.imf.org/2021/06/18/a-proposal-to-scale-up-global-carbon-pricing.

55 Bank of England, "Key elements of the 2021 Biennial Exploratory Scenario: Financial risks from climate

change", 8 June 2021, https://www.bankofengland.co.uk/stress-testing/2021/key-elements-2021-biennial-exploratory-scenario-financial-risks-climate-change.

56 *The Economist*, "A third of Americans deny human-caused climate change exists", 8 July 2021, https://www.economist.com/graphic-detail/2021/07/08/a-third-of-americans-deny-human-caused-climate-change-exists.

57 David Sharp, "Mainers vote to halt $1B electric transmission line", AP News, 3 November 2021, https://apnews.com/article/election-2021-maine-hydropower-line-54dea1a948e9fc57a667280707cddeb7.

58 Kantar Public, "Our planet issue: Accelerating behaviour change for a sustainable future", Public Journal 04, 2021, https://kantar.turtl.co/story/public-journal-04/page/1.

59 Intergenerational inequity is much discussed, well understood and widely publicized (thanks to Greta Thunberg and some of her peers). The role of wealth inequity is a bit less – for the moment. Yet, as the UN *Emissions Gap Report 2020* states: "A range of estimates point to a strong correlation between income and emissions, with a highly unequal global distribution of consumption emissions. Such studies estimate that the emissions share of the top 10 per cent of income earners is around 36-49 per cent of the global total, whereas the lowest 50 per cent of income earners account for around 7-15 per cent of all emissions." See United Nations Environment Programme, *Emissions Gap Report 2020*, https://www.unep.org/emissions-gap-report-2020.

60 Chandran Nair makes this point in "Net Zero and Carbon Neutrality: Unscientific Myths for an US and THEM World", The Club of Rome, 18 October 2021, https://www.clubofrome.org/blog-post/nair-carbon-neutrality.

61 Simon Evans, "Analysis: Which countries are historically responsible for climate change?", CarbonBrief, 5 October 2021, https://www.carbonbrief.org/analysis-which-countries-are-historically-responsible-for-climate-change.

62 Chandran Nair, "Net Zero and Carbon Neutrality: Unscientific Myths for an US and THEM World", The Club of Rome, 18 October 2021.

63 This concept was popularized by Harvard professor Graham Allison in his book *Destined for War: Can America and China Escape Thucydides's Trap?*, Mariner Books, 2017, https://www.amazon.com/s?k=Allison+graham&i=stripbooks-intl-ship&ref=nb_sb_noss_2.

64 John J. Mearsheimer, "The Inevitable Rivalry: America, China, and the Tragedy of Great-Power Politics", *Foreign Affairs*, November/December 2021, https://www.foreignaffairs.com/articles/china/2021-10-19/inevitable-rivalry-cold-war.

65 The expression was coined by Subrahmanyam Jaishankar, an Indian foreign affairs official. See Frederik Kempe, "The US is working through a 'strategic contraction'", Heromag, 21 November 2021, https://heromag.net/the-us-is-working-through-a-strategic-contraction.

66 The Quadrilateral Security Dialogue (the Quad) between the US, India, Japan and Australia is an example of efforts to counter China's influence. It was created in 2007 and, after a pause, re-established in 2017 when it gained greater relevance.

67 Jude Blanchette, "Xi's Confidence Game: Beijing's Actions Show Determination, not Insecurity", *Foreign Affairs*, 23 November 2021, https://www.foreignaffairs.com/articles/asia/2021-11-23/xis-confidence-game.

68 See Gillian Tett, "The US and China are already at war. But which kind?", *Financial Times*, 24 November 2021, https://www.ft.com/content/583b44f7-5eb5-4967-983d-70d0f5573f5c.

69 United Nations, "Secretary-General's Nelson Mandela Lecture: 'Tackling the Inequality Pandemic: A New Social Contract for a New Era' [as delivered]", 18 July 2020, https://www.un.org/sg/en/content/sg/statement/2020-07-18/secretary-generals-nelson-mandela-lecture-%E2%80%9Ctackling-the-inequality-pandemic-new-social-contract-for-new-era%E2%80%9D-delivered.

70 Anthony Shorrocks, James Davies and Rodrigo Lluberas, *Global wealth report 2021*, Credit Suisse, Research Institute, 2021, https://www.credit-suisse.com/about-us/en/reports-research/global-wealth-report.html.

71 Lucas Chancel, Thomas Piketty, Emmanuel Saez and Gabriel Zucman (eds), *World Inequality Report 2022*, World Inequality Database (WID.world), 2021, https://wid.world/news-article/world-inequality-report-2022.

72 Income inequality could be a partial exception. In the early stages of the pandemic and in many countries, income-support programmes and other stimulus measures increased the revenues of the lowest-paid workers and households, and thereby reduced income inequality. However, this situation will probably be reversed when the support measures are phased out.

73 Marc Kadir, "Student view: Covid's legacy will be an economically more unequal world", *Financial Times*, 3 October 2021, https://www.ft.com/content/f5462084-f123-4bcf-b1a0-587b79a319b6.

74 Brooke Harrington, *Capital Without Borders: Wealth Managers and the One Percent*, Harvard University Press, 2020, https://www.amazon.com/Capital-without-Borders-Managers-Percent/dp/067424477X/ref=sr_1_1?keywords=Capital+Without+Borders%3A+Wealth+Managers+and+the+One+Percent&qid=1638022175&qsid=131-9078639-9083348&s=books&sr=1-1&sres=067424477X&srpt=ABIS_BOOK.

75 Armed Conflict Location & Event Data Project (ACLED), "A Year of COVID-19: The Pandemic's Impact on Global Conflict and Demonstration Trends", 2021, https://acleddata.com/acleddatanew/wp-content/uploads/2021/04/ACLED_A-Year-of-COVID19_April2021.pdf.

76 Manuel Rueda, "Colombia protesters: We're not scared anymore", BBC News, 14 May 2021, https://www.bbc.com/news/world-latin-america-57105000.

77 Zachariah Mampilly, "Protests Are Taking Over the World. What's Driving Them?", *The New York Times*, 3 October 2021, https://www.nytimes.com/2021/10/03/opinion/covid-protests-world-whats-driving-them.html.

78 Minouche Shafik, *What We Owe Each Other: A New Social Contract*, Penguin Random House, 2021, https://www.amazon.co.uk/What-We-Owe-Each-Other/dp/1847926274/ref=sr_1_1?keywords=minouche+shafik&qid=1639625860&s=books&sr=1-1.

79 This is shown in particular in the annual Edelman Trust Barometer, https://www.edelman.com/trustbarometer.

80 Two prominent examples emanate from the International Panel on Social Progress, *Rethinking Society for the 21st Century*, 2018, https://www.cambridge.org/gb/academic/subjects/politics-international-relations/political-economy/rethinking-society-21st-century-report-international-panel-social-progress; and Maurizio Bussolo, Maria E. Davalos, Vito Peragine and Ramya Sundarm, *Toward a New Social Contract*, World Bank, 2019, https://openknowledge.worldbank.org/bitstream/handle/10986/30393/9781464813535.pdf.

81 Henry A. Kissinger "The Coronavirus Pandemic Will Forever Alter the World Order", *The Wall Street Journal*, 3 April 2020, https://www.wsj.com/articles/the-coronavirus-pandemic-will-forever-alter-the-world-order-11585953005.

82 Katherine Hu, "'I Just Don't Think We Have the Luxury to Have Dreams Anymore'", *The New York Times*, 24 March 2020, https://www.nytimes.com/2020/03/24/opinion/coronavirus-recession-gen-z.html.

83 Jennifer McNulty, "Youth activism is on the rise around the globe, and adults should pay attention, says author", UC Santa Cruz, 17 September 2019, https://news.ucsc.edu/2019/09/taft-youth.html.

84 As an example, in September 2019, more than 4 million young people demonstrated simultaneously in 150 countries to demand urgent action on climate change. See Somini Sengupta, "Protesting Climate Change, Young People Take to Streets in a Global Strike", *The New York Times*, 20 September 2019, https://www.nytimes.com/2019/09/20/climate/global-climate-strike.html. Also, it is truly global. See Delger Erdenesanaa, "At COP26, Youth Activists From Around the World Call Out Decades of Delay", Inside Climate News, 10 November 2021, https://insideclimatenews.org/news/10112021/cop26-youth-activists.

85 Conversation with Niall Ferguson.

86 Conducted at the Leverhulme Centre for the Future of Intelligence at Cambridge University. The quotes are attributed to Kanta Dihal, who researches AI narratives. See the Leverhulme Centre for the Future of Intelligence website at http://lcfi.ac.uk/projects/ai-narratives-and-justice/global-ai-narratives.

87 Madhumita Murgia, "Into the metaverse: how sci-fi shapes our attitudes to the future", *Financial Times*, 2 November 2021, https://www.ft.com/content/2f35be37-9da8-4cf6-89b2-8488b36c5a63.

88 Isaac Asimov and Jason Shulman (eds), *Isaac Asimov's Book of Science and Nature Quotations*, Weidenfeld & Nicolson, 1988, https://www.amazon.com/Isaac-Asimovs-Science-Nature-Quotations/dp/1555844448.

89 Famous Psychologists, "Herbert Simon", https://www.famouspsychologists.org/herbert-simon.

90 In her book, *The Age of Surveillance Capitalism: The Fight for a Human Future at the New Frontier of Power*, the scholar Shoshana Zuboff warns about customers being reinvented as data sources, with surveillance capitalism transforming our economy, society, politics and our own lives by producing deeply anti-democratic asymmetries of knowledge and the power that accrues to knowledge (PublicAffairs, 2020, https://www.amazon.com/Age-Surveillance-Capitalism-Future-Frontier/dp/1541758005/ref=sr_1_1?keywords=the+age+of+surveillance+capitalism&qid=1639689529&s=books&sr=1-1).

91 In *The Age of AI And Our Human Future*, a statesman (Henry Kissinger), the former CEO of Google (Eric Schmidt) and a computer scientist (Daniel Huttenlocher) argue that AI will challenge the primacy of human reason that has existed since the dawn of the Enlightenment (Little, Brown and Company, 2021, https://www.amazon.com/gp/product/0316273805?tag=hacboogrosit-20).

92 Steve Morgan, "Cybercrime To Cost The World $10.5 Trillion Annually By 2025", *Cybercrime Magazine*, 13 November 2020, https://cybersecurityventures.com/cybercrime-damages-6-trillion-by-2021.

93 Marietje Schaake, "The Lawless Realm, Countering the Real Cyberthreat", *Foreign Affairs*, November/December 2020, https://www.foreignaffairs.com/articles/world/2020-10-13/lawless-realm.

94 D. Howard Kass, "500 Million Attempted Ransomware Attacks (So Far) In 2021", MSSP Alert, 1 November 2021, https://www.msspalert.com/cybersecurity-research/500-million-attempted-ransomware-attacks-so-far-in-2021.

95 Joe Hernandez, "A Military Drone With A Mind Of Its Own Was Used In Combat, U.N. Says", NPR, 1 June 2021, https://www.npr.org/2021/06/01/1002196245/a-u-n-report-suggests-libya-saw-the-first-battlefield-killing-by-an-autonomous-d.

96 Madhumita Murgia, "AI weapons pose threat to humanity, warns top scientist", *Financial Times*, 29 November 2021, https://www.ft.com/content/03b2c443-b839-4093-a8f0-968987f426f4.

97 Future of Life Institute [website], https://futureoflife.org.

98 AI Scientists 4 Peace, "Stop the arming of drones for the Bundeswehr – outlaw autonomous weapon systems!", https://aiscientists4peace.org/offener-brief/english-version.

99 Joseph S. Nye, "It's not too late to exert human control over artificial intelligence, this book argues",

Project Syndicate, 7 December 2021, https://www.marketwatch.com/story/its-not-too-late-to-exert-human-control-over-artificial-intelligence-this-book-argues-11638382862.

100 Jamie Metzl, "Miraculous mRNA Vaccines are only the Beginning", *Newsweek*, 12 February 2021, https://www.newsweek.com/miraculous-mrna-vaccines-are-only-beginning-opinion-1567683.

101 Quoted by Jamie Metzl during our conversation.

102 Conversation with John Steele.

103 Conversation with Jamie Metzl. This dilemma is explored in depth in his book, *Hacking Darwin: Genetic Engineering and the Future of Humanity* (Sourcebooks, 2020, https://www.amazon.com/Hacking-Darwin-Genetic-Engineering-Humanity/dp/1728214130/ref=sr_1_fkmr1_1?keywords=James+Metzl+hacking+darwin&qid=1639118263&s=books&sr=1-1-fkmr1).

104 Martin Wolf, "How we can share our divided world?", *Financial Times*, 2 November 2021, https://www.ft.com/content/b371e181-eac3-41ef-88c5-ca2bb20edd99.

105 Richard Davidson, "Innate basic goodness", Innerchange, https://innerchange.life/peace-media-library/richard-davidson-innate-basic-goodness.

106 John Hesch, "Fostering the development of compassion in young children", *Pastoral Psychology*, vol. 41, 1992, pp. 31-37, https://link.springer.com/article/10.1007/BF01054775.

107 F. Diane Barth, "Can Empathy Be Taught?", *Psychology Today*, 18 October 2018, https://www.psychologytoday.com/us/blog/the-couch/201810/can-empathy-be-taught.

108 John F. Helliwell, et al. (eds), *World Happiness Report*, 2020, https://worldhappiness.report/ed/2020/#read.

109 Jessica Alexander, "America's Insensitive Children?", *The Atlantic*, 9 August 2016, https://www.theatlantic.com/education/archive/2016/08/the-us-empathy-gap/494975.

110 Richard J Davidson, "About Richard J. Davidson", https://www.richardjdavidson.com/about; and Richard Davidson, "Change your brain, change the world", Innerchange, https://innerchange.life/peace-media-library/richard-davidson-change-your-brain-change-the-world.

111 Martin Wolf, "How we can share our divided world", *Financial Times*, 2 November 2021.

112 United "Nations, *Our Common Agenda, Report of the Secretary-General*, United Nations, 2021, https://www.un.org/en/content/common-agenda-report/assets/pdf/Common_Agenda_Report_English.pdf.

113 Merriam-Webster, "imagination" definition, https://www.merriam-webster.com/dictionary/imagination.

114 Graham Greene used it in a slightly different context, that of negative emotions: "Hate was just a failure of imagination." But his expression now sticks.

115 Caleb A. Scharf, "A Failure of Imagination", *Scientific American*, 14 May 2020, https://blogs.scientificamerican.com/life-unbounded/a-failure-of-imagination.

116 David Graeber and David Wengrow, *The Dawn of Everything: A New History of Humanity*, Farrar, Straus and Giroux, 2021, https://www.amazon.com/Dawn-Everything-New-History-Humanity/dp/0374157359.

117 Network for Greening the Financial System (NGFS), *Adapting central bank operations to a hotter world: Reviewing some options*, 2021, https://www.ngfs.net/sites/default/files/media/2021/06/17/ngfs_monetary_policy_operations_final.pdf.

118 Network for Greening the Financial System (NGFS), *NGFS Climate Scenarios for central banks and supervisors*, 2021, https://www.ngfs.net/sites/default/files/media/2021/08/27/ngfs_climate_scenarios_phase2_june2021.pdf.

119 The nine main options for adjusting operational frameworks to climate-related risks are summarized in the NGFS report *Adapting central bank operations to a hotter world: Reviewing some options*, 2021, Table 1, p. 5.

120 Most notably, Delton Chen, Joel van der Beek and Jonathan Cloud, "Climate mitigation policy as a system solution: addressing the risk cost of carbon", *Journal of Sustainable Finance & Investment*, vol. 7, no. 3, 2017, https://www.tandfonline.com/doi/abs/10.1080/20430795.2017.1314814; and Delton Chen, Joel van der Beek and Jonathan Cloud, "Hypothesis for a Risk Cost of

Carbon: Revising the Externalities and Ethics of Climate Change", in H. Doukas, A. Flamos and J. Lieu (eds), *Understanding Risks and Uncertainties in Energy and Climate Policy*, Springer Nature, 2018, https://rd.springer.com/chapter/10.1007/978-3-030-03152-7_8.

121 Kim Stanley Robinson, "A climate plan for a world in flames", *Financial Times*, 20 August 2021, https://www.ft.com/content/ff94df96-b702-4e01-addd-f4253d0eecf6.

122 Frank Van Gansbeke, "Time For IMF Climate Coin (1/3)", *Forbes*, 17 January 2021, https://www.forbes.com/sites/frankvangansbeke/2021/01/17/time-for-imf-climate-coin-13/?sh=673c2ae8401d.

123 Nature4Climate, "The Global Value of Nature", https://nature4climate.org/the-global-value-of-nature.

124 A good summary is provided in the webinar "Valuing Nature: Whales, Elephants, and the Global Economy", Institute for International Economic Policy, 2020, https://iiep.gwu.edu/2020/11/12/valuing-nature-whales-elephants-and-the-global-economy. The Dasgupta Review is the most authoritative official report on the subject of natural capital. It is the equivalent on nature and biodiversity to *The Stern Review* on climate change of 2006. See Gov.UK, "Final Report – The Economics of Biodiversity: The Dasgupta Review", 20 August 2021 update, https://www.gov.uk/government/publications/final-report-the-economics-of-biodiversity-the-dasgupta-review.

125 Gov.UK, "The Economics of Biodiversity: The Dasgupta Review – Headline Messages", 2021, https://assets.publishing.service.gov.uk/government/uploads/system/uploads/attachment_data/file/957629/Dasgupta_Review_-_Headline_Messages.pdf.

126 This is not based on a rigorous analysis of the landscape but is grounded in observational evidence provided by the "good4nature" prize. See Monthly Barometer, "good4nature: an international prize for a nature-positive economy", 2021, https://monthlybarometer.com/wp-content/uploads/2021/05/GOOD4NATURE.pdf.

127 Food and Agriculture Organization of the United Nations (FAO), "How Sustainability Is Addressed in Official Bioeconomy Strategies at International, National and Regional Levels", Environment and Natural Resources Management Working Paper, 2016, p.1, https://www.fao.org/3/i5998e/i5998e.pdf.

128 Schmidt Futures, *Public and Private Funding Opportunities to Advance a Circular U.S. Bioeconomy and Maintain U.S. Biotechnology Competitiveness*, Interim Report Informed by the Schmidt Futures Bioeconomy Task Force, 1 December 2021, https://schmidtfutures.com/wp-content/uploads/Bioeconomy-Task-Force-Interim-Report-12.1.21.pdf.

129 David King and Jane Lichtenstein, "The need for Climate Repair: A plan for surviving and thriving", Centre for Climate Repair at Cambridge, Downing College, https://www.climaterepair.cam.ac.uk/files/jane_dave.pdf; and, more generally, University of

Cambridge, "Centre for Climate Repair at Cambridge", https://www.climaterepair.cam.ac.uk.
130 Gernot Wagner, *Geoengineering: The Gamble*, Polity, 2021, https://www.amazon.co.uk/s?k=gernot+wagner&i=stripbooks&crid=KD3F3E89A2V5&sprefix=gernot+%2Cstripbooks%2C173&ref=nb_sb_ss_ts-doa-p_1_7.
131 Conversation with Patricia Churchland.
132 Conversation with Rana Foroohar.
133 Conversation with Branko Milanovic.
134 Chandran Nair, *Dismantling Global White Privilege: Equity for a Post-Western World*, Berrett-Koehler Publishers, 2022, https://www.amazon.com/Dismantling-Global-White-Privilege-Post-Western/dp/1523000007.
135 United Nations, "Universal Declaration of Human Rights", Approved by the General Assembly at its Plenary Meeting on 10 December 1948, https://www.un.org/sites/un2.un.org/files/udhr.pdf.
136 Conversation with Amie Thomasson.
137 Diane Coyle, "Change is needed in the next generation of economists", *Financial Times*, 4 October 2021, https://www.ft.com/content/1ec4a6c3-b5db-4e9b-ab48-573541b9676b.
138 Conversation with Diane Coyle.
139 Damian Carrington, "Climate crisis: economists 'grossly undervalue young lives', warns Stern", *The Guardian*, 25 October 2021, https://www.theguardian.com/environment/2021/oct/26/climate-crisis-economists-grossly-undervalue-young-lives-warns-stern.

140 Nicholas Stern, "A time for action on climate change and a time for change in economics", Centre for Climate Change Economics and Policy Working Paper 397/Grantham Research Institute on Climate Change and the Environment Working Paper 370, 2021, https://www.lse.ac.uk/granthaminstitute/wp-content/uploads/2021/10/working-paper-370-Stern.pdf.

141 Guido Tabellini, "Morality matters for economic performance", VOXeu, 22 December 2007, https://voxeu.org/article/does-morality-affect-economic-performance-empirical-evidence.

142 The University of Chicago Booth School of Business, "Luigi Zingales, Robert C. McCormack Distinguished Service Professor of Entrepreneurship and Finance and George G. Rinder Faculty Fellow", 2021, https://www.chicagobooth.edu/faculty/directory/z/luigi-zingales.

143 Conversation with Rebecca Henderson. Her argument is developed in *Reimagining Capitalism in a World on Fire*, Penguin, 2021, https://www.amazon.com/Reimagining-Capitalism-World-Fire/dp/0241379687/ref=tmm_pap_swatch_0?_encoding=UTF8&qid=1638797612&sr=1-1.

144 Mark Carney, *Value(s): Building a Better World For All*, PublicAffairs, 2021, https://www.amazon.com/Value-Building-Better-World-All/dp/1541768701.

145 The political philosopher Michael Sandel has theorized the notion that some countries like the US have moved from a "market economy" to a "market society". See

Michael Sandel, "What Isn't for Sale?", *The Atlantic*, April 2012, https://www.theatlantic.com/magazine/archive/2012/04/what-isnt-for-sale/308902.

146 Robert A. Huber, Esther Greussing and Jakob-Moritz Eberl, "From populism to climate scepticism: the role of institutional trust and attitudes towards science", *Environmental Politics*, 24 September 2021, https://www.tandfonline.com/doi/full/10.1080/09644016.2021.1978200.

147 Sania Nishtar, "Climate Policy Is Social Policy", Project Syndicate, 4 November 2021, https://www.project-syndicate.org/commentary/right-climate-fight-poverty-by-sania-nishtar-2021-11.

148 This is changing, but only recently has economics started to take seriously into consideration the contribution of natural and social capital to growth and development.

149 United Nations, Sustainable Development, "The 17 Goals", https://sdgs.un.org/goals.

150 Nicholas Stern, "A time for action on climate change and a time for change in economics", Centre for Climate Change Economics and Policy Working Paper 397/Grantham Research Institute on Climate Change and the Environment Working Paper 370, 2021, https://www.lse.ac.uk/granthaminstitute/wp-content/uploads/2021/10/working-paper-370-Stern.pdf.

151 European Commission, "A European Green Deal", https://ec.europa.eu/info/strategy/priorities-2019-2024/european-green-deal_en.

152 Lorna Hutchinson, "'Europe's man on the moon moment': Von der Leyen unveils EU Green Deal", *The Parliament Magazine*, 11 December 2019, https://www.theparliamentmagazine.eu/news/article/europes-man-on-the-moon-moment-von-der-leyen-unveils-eu-green-deal.

153 European Parliament, "Europe's one trillion climate finance plan", News, 25 June 2021 update, https://www.europarl.europa.eu/news/en/headlines/society/20200109STO69927/europe-s-one-trillion-climate-finance-plan.

154 European Parliament, "A Just Transition Fund – How the EU budget can best assist in the necessary transition from fossil fuels to sustainable energy", Policy Department for Budgetary Affairs, Directorate General for Internal Policies of the Union, 2020, https://www.bruegel.org/wp-content/uploads/2020/05/Bruegel-JTF-report-for-EP-BUDG2.pdf.

155 Organisation for Economic Co-operation and Development (OECD), "Economic policies to foster green growth", 2021, https://www.oecd.org/greengrowth/greeneco.

156 European Commission, "Press remarks by President von der Leyen on the occasion of the adoption of the European Green Deal Communication", 11 December 2019, https://ec.europa.eu/commission/presscorner/detail/fr/speech_19_6749.

157 Jean Pisani-Ferry, "21-20 Climate Policy is Macroeconomic Policy, and the Implications Will Be Significant",

Peterson Institute for International Economics (PIIE), 2021, https://www.piie.com/system/files/documents/pb21-20.pdf.

158 Vitor Gaspar and Ian Parry, "A Proposal to Scale Up Global Carbon Pricing", International Monetary Fund, IMFBlog, 18 June 2021, https://blogs.imf.org/2021/06/18/a-proposal-to-scale-up-global-carbon-pricing; Bank of England, "Key elements of the 2021 Biennial Exploratory Scenario: Financial risks from climate change", 8 June 2021, https://www.bankofengland.co.uk/stress-testing/2021/key-elements-2021-biennial-exploratory-scenario-financial-risks-climate-change.

159 This pre-COVID article makes it clear that social activism and demonstrations are "only the beginning": Matthew Taylor, Jonathan Watts and John Bartlett, "Climate crisis: 6 million people join latest wave of global protests", *The Guardian*, 27 September 2019, https://www.theguardian.com/environment/2019/sep/27/climate-crisis-6-million-people-join-latest-wave-of-worldwide-protests.

160 Conversation with Chandran Nair.

161 Margaret Thatcher Foundation, "Interview for *Woman's Own*", Thatcher Archive, 23 September 1987, https://www.margaretthatcher.org/document/106689.

162 Mariana Mazzucato, "The Covid-19 crisis is a chance to do capitalism differently", *The Guardian*, 18 March 2020, https://www.theguardian.com/commentisfree/2020/mar/18/the-covid-19-crisis-is-a-chance-to-do-capitalism-differently.

163 Joseph Stiglitz, "A Lasting Remedy for the Covid-19 Pandemic's Economic Crisis", *The New York Review of Books*, 8 April 2020, https://www.nybooks.com/daily/2020/04/08/a-lasting-remedy-for-the-covid-19-pandemics-economic-crisis.

164 European Commission, "Recovery plan for Europe", 2020, https://ec.europa.eu/info/strategy/recovery-plan-europe_en.

165 Takatoshi Ito, "Beware of Japan's 'New Capitalism'", Project Syndicate, 19 November 2021, https://www.project-syndicate.org/commentary/new-capitalism-under-kishida-is-plain-old-socialism-by-takatoshi-ito-2021-11.

166 Conversation with Raghuram Rajan.

167 Conversation with Mariana Mazzucato.

168 Mariana Mazzucato, "The Creative State", Project Syndicate, 16 April 2015, https://www.project-syndicate.org/commentary/government-investment-innovation-by-mariana-mazzucato-2015-04.

169 Markus Brunnermeier, *The Resilient Society*, Endeavor Literary Press, 2021, https://www.amazon.com/Resilient-Society-Markus-Brunnermeier/dp/1737403609/ref=tmm_pap_swatch_0?_encoding=UTF8&qid=1637398883&sr=8-1.

170 Peter Coy, "How a Princeton Economist Teaches Resilience", *The New York Times*, 27 September 2021, https://www.nytimes.com/2021/09/27/opinion/resilience-princeton-economist.html.

171 Markus Brunnermeier, *The Resilient Society*, Endeavor Literary Press, 2021.

172 UK Government, G7 United Kingdom 2021, "Economic Resilience Panel", 13 October 2021, https://www.g7uk.org/economic-resilience-panel.

173 UK Government, G7 Panel on Economic Resilience, *Global Economic Resilience: Building Forward Better*, 2021, https://www.g7uk.org/wp-content/uploads/2021/10/G7-Economic-Resilience-Panel-Report.pdf.

174 James Manyika, et al., "A new look at how corporations impact the economy and households", McKinsey & Company, Discussion Paper, 31 May 2021, https://www.mckinsey.com/business-functions/strategy-and-corporate-finance/our-insights/a-new-look-at-how-corporations-impact-the-economy-and-households.

175 Milton Friedman, "A Friedman doctrine – The Social Responsibility Of Business Is to Increase Its Profits", *The New York Times*, 13 September 1970, https://www.nytimes.com/1970/09/13/archives/a-friedman-doctrine-the-social-responsibility-of-business-is-to.html.

176 Ibid.

177 Klaus Schwab, "Davos Manifesto 1973: A Code of Ethics for Business Leaders", World Economic Forum Agenda, 2 December 2019, https://www.weforum.org/agenda/2019/12/davos-manifesto-1973-a-code-of-ethics-for-business-leaders.

178 Gordon Gekko in the film *Wall Street* (1987), a powerful narrative that perfectly captures the atmosphere of these years.

179 These numbers are cited in Diane Coyle, "The Revolution Will Not Be Privatized: Corporate Responsibility and Its Limits", *Foreign Affairs*, January/February 2022, https://www.foreignaffairs.com/articles/world/2021-12-14/revolution-will-not-be-privatized.

180 Business Roundtable, "Business Roundtable Redefines the Purpose of a Corporation to Promote 'An Economy That Serves All Americans'", 19 August 2019, https://www.businessroundtable.org/business-roundtable-redefines-the-purpose-of-a-corporation-to-promote-an-economy-that-serves-all-americans.

181 Alan Murray, "America's CEOs Seek a New Purpose for the Corporation", *Fortune*, 19 August 2019, https://fortune.com/longform/business-roundtable-ceos-corporations-purpose.

182 Klaus Schwab, "Davos Manifesto 2020: The Universal Purpose of a Company in the Fourth Industrial Revolution", World Economic Forum Agenda, 2 December 2019, https://www.weforum.org/agenda/2019/12/davos-manifesto-2020-the-universal-purpose-of-a-company-in-the-fourth-industrial-revolution.

183 US President Reagan famously said, "The nine most terrifying words in the English language are: I'm from the government and I'm here to help". See Ronald Reagan Presidential Foundation and Institute, "Reagan Quotes

and Speeches", 12 August 1986, https://www.reaganfoundation.org/ronald-reagan/reagan-quotes-speeches/news-conference-1.

184 World Economic Forum in collaboration with Deloitte, EY, KPMG and PwC, "Measuring Stakeholder Capitalism: Towards Common Metrics and Consistent Reporting of Sustainable Value Creation", White Paper, 2020, https://www3.weforum.org/docs/WEF_IBC_Measuring_Stakeholder_Capitalism_Report_2020.pdf.

185 Colm Kelly and Dennis J. Snower, "Capitalism recoupled", *Oxford Review of Economic Policy*, vol. 37, no. 4, Winter 2021, pp. 851-863, https://academic.oup.com/oxrep/article/37/4/851/6423485.

186 Kearney, "Shareholder vs stakeholder value: CEO debate", World Economic Forum session, https://www.kearney.com/web/world-economic-forum/shareholder-vs-stakeholder-value.

187 The ability of Engine No. 1, an activist hedge fund, to get two seats on the Exxon board while having a stake in the company of just 0.02% is a remarkable manifestation of this trend. See Clifford Krauss, "Exxon Board to Get a Third Activist Pushing Cleaner Energy", *The New York Times*, 9 June 2021 update, https://www.nytimes.com/2021/06/02/business/exxon-board-clean-energy.html.

188 Klaus Schwab, "Global Corporate Citizenship", *Foreign Affairs*, January/February 2008, https://ciaotest.cc.columbia.edu/journals/fa/v87i1/0000792.pdf.

189 Klaus Schwab, "Capitalism Must Reform to Survive: From Shareholders to Stakeholders", *Foreign Affairs*, 16 January 2020, https://www.foreignaffairs.com/articles/2020-01-16/capitalism-must-reform-survive.

190 Azeem Azhar, *The Exponential Age: How Accelerating Technology is Transforming Business, Politics and Society*, Diversion Books, 2021, https://diversionbooks.com/books/the-exponential-age.

191 Zoë Corbyn, "Peter Diamandis: 'In the next 10 years, we'll reinvent every industry'", *The Guardian*, 25 January 2020, https://www.theguardian.com/technology/2020/jan/25/peter-diamandis-future-faster-think-interview-ai-industry. Peter Diamandis makes the same argument about accelerating/exponential change as Azeem Azhar in *The Future Is Faster Than You Think: How Converging Technologies Are Transforming Business, Industries, and Our Lives* (Exponential Technology Series), Simon & Schuster, 2020.

192 Conversation with Michio Kaku.

193 SYSTEMIQ, "The Paris Effect: How the Climate Agreement Is Reshaping the Global Economy", 9 December 2020, https://www.systemiq.earth/paris-effect.

194 This point is made in a report published by the Institute for New Economic Thinking (INET) at the Oxford Martin School: *A new perspective on decarbonising the global energy system*, 2021, https://www.inet.ox.ac.uk/news/report-a-new-perspective-on-decarbonising-the-global-energy-system.

195 These assertions are made in the report referenced in the previous endnote and in various analyses conducted by the INET Oxford Complexity Economics team ("INET Oxford's programmes, Complexity Economics: Overview", https://www.inet.ox.ac.uk/research/programmes/complexity-economics). Their conclusions are also embraced by the authoritative Energy Transitions Commission. See in particular "Keeping 1.5°C Alive: Closing the Gap in the 2020s", Executive Summary, 2021, https://www.energy-transitions.org/wp-content/uploads/2021/09/ETC-Keeping-1.5C-Alive-Closing-the-Gap-in-the-2020s-Executive-Summary.pdf.

196 Institute for New Economic Thinking, "Report: 'A new perspective on decarbonising the global energy system'", 19 April 2021, https://www.inet.ox.ac.uk/news/report-a-new-perspective-on-decarbonising-the-global-energy-system.

197 Energy Transitions Commission, "Our ambition", 2021, https://www.energy-transitions.org/ambition.

198 International Energy Agency (IEA), "Renewable electricity growth is accelerating faster than ever worldwide, supporting the emergence of the new global energy economy", Press release, 1 December 2021, https://www.iea.org/news/renewable-electricity-growth-is-accelerating-faster-than-ever-worldwide-supporting-the-emergence-of-the-new-global-energy-economy.

199 Ibid.

200 Klaus Schwab, *The Fourth Industrial Revolution*, Currency, 2017, https://www.amazon.com/Fourth-Industrial-Revolution-Klaus-Schwab/dp/1524758868/ref=tmm_hrd_swatch_0?_encoding=UTF8&qid=1639156166&sr=8-1.

201 Designer and architect Neri Oxman offers a fascinating example of this. Her research lab works at the intersection of computational design, additive manufacturing, materials engineering and synthetic biology. See TED, Ideas worth spreading, "Neri Oxman, Design at the intersection of technology and biology", 2015, https://www.ted.com/talks/neri_oxman_design_at_the_intersection_of_technology_and_biology.

202 Erik Brynjolfsson and Andrew McAfee, *The Second Machine Age: Work, Progress, and Prosperity in a Time of Brilliant Technologies*, W.W. Norton & Company, 2014, https://www.amazon.com/Second-Machine-Age-Prosperity-Technologies/dp/0393239357/ref=tmm_hrd_swatch_0?_encoding=UTF8&qid=1639201006&sr=1-1.

203 Drew Endy, a professor of bioengineering at Stanford University, quoted in "Can Synthetic Biology Save Us? This Scientist Thinks So", *The New York Times*, 23 November 2021, https://www.nytimes.com/2021/11/23/business/dealbook/synthetic-biology-drew-endy.html.

204 Conversation with Jennifer Doudna.

205 International Genetically Engineered Machine (iGEM), "Welcome to the iGEM 2021 Competition Website", https://2021.igem.org/Main_Page.

206 SynBioBeta, "2Q 2021 Synthetic Biology Venture Investment Report", 6 October 2021, https://synbiobeta.com/2q-2021-synthetic-biology-venture-investment-report.

207 McKinsey & Company, "The top trends in tech", 2021, https://www.mckinsey.com/business-functions/mckinsey-digital/our-insights/the-top-trends-in-tech.

208 World Economic Forum, in collaboration with the UC Berkeley Center for Human-Compatible AI and Roland Berger, *Positive AI Economic Futures*, Insight Report, 2021, https://www3.weforum.org/docs/WEF_Positive_AI_Economic_Futures_2021.pdf.

209 Conversation with Raghuram Rajan.

210 Steven Pinker, *The Better Angels of Our Nature: A History of Violence and Humanity*, Penguin, 2012, https://www.amazon.co.uk/Better-Angels-Our-Nature-Violence/dp/0141034645/ref=sr_1_5?keywords=pinker&qid=1637136175&s=books&sr=1-5.

211 Steven Pinker, *Enlightenment Now: The Case for Reason, Science, Humanism, and Progress*, Viking, 2018, https://www.amazon.com/Enlightenment-Now-Science-Humanism-Progress/dp/0525427570.

212 Hans Rosling, Ola Rosling and Anna Rosling Rönnlund, *Factfulness: Ten Reasons We're Wrong About The World - And Why Things Are Better Than You Think*, Sceptre, 2018, https://www.amazon.co.uk/Factfulness-Reasons-Wrong-Things-Better/dp/1473637465/ref=tmm_hrd_swatch_0?_encoding=UTF8&qid=1637136426&sr=1-1.

213 Wired, "Barack Obama: Now Is the Greatest Time to Be Alive", 18 December 2016, https://www.wired.com/2016/10/president-obama-guest-edits-wired-essay.

214 Michel Serres, *C'était mieux avant!* (*It was better before!*), Pommier [in French], 2017, https://www.amazon.com/C%C3%A9tait-mieux-avant/dp/2746512882.

215 Jean Twenge, "The Sad State of Happiness in the United States and the Role of Digital Media", in *World Happiness Report 2019*, Chapter 5, 20 March 2019, https://worldhappiness.report/ed/2019/the-sad-state-of-happiness-in-the-united-states-and-the-role-of-digital-media.

216 Yuval Noah Harari and Steven Pinker in conversation, moderated by Maksym Yakovlyev, YouTube, September 2019, https://www.youtube.com/watch?v=qHSzeijQ95I.

217 LibQuotes, Leo Tolstoy, "Three Methods of Reform" in *Pamphlets* [in Russian], 1900.

218 Edward Everett Hale, *Lend a Hand*, c. 1871, in Margaret Miner and Hugh Rawson (eds), *The Oxford Dictionary of American Quotations*, Second Edition, Oxford University Press, 2006.

219 In a speech delivered in 2001. However, this quote has also been attributed to many leaders and thinkers, among them Seneca, Napoleon, Churchill, Disraeli, Burke and others.

Printed in Poland
by Amazon Fulfillment
Poland Sp. z o.o., Wrocław

85501201R00143